THE
ETHICAL
INVESTOR

THE
ETHICAL
INVESTOR

Making Gains With Values

＊

JOHN HANCOCK

PEARSON EDUCATION LIMITED

Head Office:
Edinburgh Gate
Harlow CM20 2JE
Tel: +44 (0)1279 623623
Fax: +44 (0)1279 431059

London Office:
128 Long Acre, London WC2E 9AN
Tel: +44 (0)171 447 2000
Fax: +44 (0)171 240 5771
www.business-minds.com

First published in Great Britain 1999

© Pearson Education Limited 1999

The right of John Hancock to be identified as author
of this work has been asserted by him in accordance
with the Copyright, Designs, and Patents Act 1988.

ISBN 0 273 63299 X

British Library Cataloguing in Publication Data
A CIP catalogue record for this book can be obtained
from the British Library.

1 3 5 7 9 10 8 6 4 2

Typeset by M Rules
Printed and bound in Great Britain by
Biddles Ltd, Guildford & King's Lynn

*The Publishers' policy is to use paper manufactured
from sustainable forests.*

ABOUT THE AUTHOR

Born 1949, John Hancock grew up in a Great Britain recovering from the massive costs of war, not sure of its place in a changing world and seemingly facing a steady decline in everything from productivity to standards of behaviour. Educated in Hampton Grammar, in his then home town of Twickenham, he went on to be an early business studies graduate, first entering the world of banking and then financial services. In 11 years with Abbey Life, John Hancock moved from field agent to development manager before joining Providence Capitol (now Old Mutual) as head of training and development. This role extended overseas and John has also headed one of the sales regions in the company before joining Citibank Financial Services as sales director. Later positions included managing director of an international financial training business, Mondial, and a regional head for Sun Life's direct sales business. Consultancies for Citibank and Hill Samuel Financial Services rounded off a career of more than 20 years in financial services.

In the early 1990s, with recession affecting the middle classes of London and the south John Hancock was offered an unpremeditated opportunity to reconsider the direction of his life in the form of redundancy. Once the initial shock had worn off, it became clear that it offered the chance to step off the increasingly treadmill like world of management work in the financial sector.

Writing had always been a passion and a pastime so it seemed very natural to turn to that as a long term possibility for work. John Hancock is now an established, working freelance journalist. This book represents a considered reflection on accumulated experience as well as the simple intellectual realisation that, stripped of its more extreme manifestations, an alternative way of doing things can work very well – for everybody.

In the mid 1990s, John Hancock and his family moved to St. Ives in Cornwall and John now works from an office overlooking the sea. It is by no means a retirement and there are times when the rate of work seems little different from those days in the city.

The Author is a member of Mensa and was awarded BESMA Journalist of the Year 1995.

GAIN ALL YOU CAN

BUT NOT AT THE EXPENSE OF YOUR CONSCIENCE

NOT AT THE EXPENSE OF OUR NEIGHBOUR'S WEALTH

NOT AT THE EXPENSE OF OUR NEIGHBOUR'S HEALTH

The titles given to four consecutive addresses by John Wesley

CONTENTS

....

Part 2
HOW DO I BECOME A CONCERNED INVESTOR?

Part 3
HOW THE PROFESSIONALS DO IT

Part 4
CURRENT AND FUTURE OUTLOOK FOR
CONCERNED INVESTMENT

Contents

Part 5

DIRECTORY OF FUNDS AND INDEPENDENT
FINANCIAL ADVISERS

FOREWORD

....

In *The Ethical Investor* John Hancock progresses well beyond the title indicated. In addition he provides us with a challenging and absorbing study of many of the ethical and environmental problems facing society today. At the same time he has carried out an in-depth research of the criteria, strategy and financial aspects of those who have become specialists in the provision of ethical financial services.

For the individual investor John Hancock outlines the choice available in the Ethical Unit Trust sector of the day and adequately emphasizes the belief that any investment made now is an investment for the future in both financial and environmental terms. He shows a recognition of the dilemmas which are inherent in any socially responsible investment policy (for example, research into a cure for AIDS or a ban on animal testing?). Such issues he discusses in an open and unprejudiced manner recognizing that within the diversity of company activities and the interests of individual investors there exist differing perceptions, philosophies, and ambitions which need to be balanced to satisfy the needs of both the stated criteria and the requirements of the investor.

The ethical movement has come a long way since those early days when the Authorities were reluctant to give permission for the establishment of a Fund which linked social concerns to investment policy. Additional resources and sophistication have now resulted in increased pressure being placed on companies to adopt a more caring and concerned attitude in their operations. It is to be hoped that the time is not far distant when all companies will not only have an effective Environmental Statement but will see the wisdom of operating in an ethical manner to providers, staff and customers alike.

Ethical investment is now both the fastest growing sector of the Unit Trust Industry and of increasing concern to institutional investors. It has surely proved by its growth and financial performance that it has truly arrived as a major investment force in the UK. John Hancock is to be thanked for his part in helping this process forward in such an interesting fashion.

CHARLES JACOB

Charles Jacob MBE was the former Investment Manager to the Methodist Church and originator of the Stewardship Unit Trust, the first Ethical Trust launched in the UK by Friends Provident in 1984. He served for 14 years on its Committee of Reference and is currently a Director of the F-P Ethical Investment Trust and Chair of its Environmental Funds Committee. For many years a Director of UKSIF, he remains a Patron.

INTRODUCTION

....

Until June 1996, I knew little and cared less about ethical, ecological or socially responsible investment. More than two decades in the financial services industry had familiarized me with what I then believed were the mainstream investment sectors but those did not include funds whose investment criteria stepped beyond the bounds of value measured as growth and profit. Even in my second career as a journalist, although I had heard about funds whose definition of a decent return embraced morality and sustainability as well as purely financial understandings, I had not been overwhelmed by the rush for articles on the topic and so had not made any effort to research it particularly. However, in June 1996, Janet Walford, the editor of *Money Management*, asked me to research and write about a still unfamiliar group of funds whose managers included in their investment criteria matters of conscience, decency and sustainability. We called the article 'The Green Maze', because of the seemingly complex matrix of considerations that make up a socially responsible investment policy. Also, reflecting the scepticism that still surrounded the sector, the opening lines read, 'Ethical funds sound good in theory, but people's ideas of what constitutes "ethical" differ widely. John Hancock looks at the performance of ethical funds to see if being green helps or hinders performance.' Those two sentences summed up the view of the general public, or those of the general public who held any view on the matter at all, that ethical investment was both complex and a version of charitable giving through investment and saving.

Several things surprised me while writing the article. In the first place, the number of green funds was many more than I had anticipated (albeit that some management groups ran several funds for several investment types). The second revelation was that the overall performance of socially responsible funds was, by that time, little different from that of any group of funds. The third surprise was that there was then, and still is, no ethical fund sector as such. Most ethical, ecological and socially responsible funds fall into one of the equity sectors. Last, but by no means least, I discovered that some fund managers actually felt that socially accountable businesses could attract a premium once it was recognized that their far-sightedness and skill at creating profit from added value rather than from depleting a finite resource or exploiting workers, suppliers and customers was a management strength. In all of this discovery and in interviewing those involved with the sector, I sensed a growing awareness that here was a movement which understood a fundamental truth of life: if you want to bring about real change, you must have control of the purse strings that govern the finances of the area within which change is desired. I also discovered a movement that was putting sound views on the future and sustainability into practice as investment criteria. Since then, I have written a number of articles on the subject and find that it is a topic in increasing demand.

To be fair, some of the early views on ethical investment were far from positive. City wags dubbed Friends Provident's first ethical fund, the Stewardship Fund, launched in 1984, the 'Brazil' fund not because of the location of its investments but because it was considered nutty! Early performance and reliability were hampered by the high proportion of small businesses in the average ethical/ecological fund portfolio – this was because such criteria were even more novel in business practices in the post-1980s commercial environment than they were in the world of investment. However, as the successful ethical businesses have thrived and as some of the world's largest businesses have embraced a socially responsible outlook, ethical funds have been able to select their stocks from an ever-broadening universe of businesses and increasing numbers of large and global organizations that meet the ethical and ecological criteria. This has enabled ethical funds to equal and, in some cases, exceed the performance of their general investment sectors.

In that time, I think that socially responsible investors have changed and some new people have come to the concept to make it less a protest movement and more an investment philosophy which, while not wanting to lose money today, allows management teams the opportunity to think, plan and act for long-term success, sustainable success. However, the themes that have shone through the history of ethical investment remain the same themes of decency, honesty, consideration and adding real value that were derived from the strong religious beliefs of early proponents of the idea. It is certainly of value to the world of business to know that there are investors who will not cast their eyes directly to the bottom line but will also be concerned with the methods by which that bottom line figure was achieved and the programmes that are in place to ensure that the bottom line will remain healthy into the future. That business values the presence of ethical investors can be seen in the increasing numbers of corporate bodies who wish to be seen to be doing the right thing in the long term and do not wish to make themselves vulnerable to aggressive take-over actions in the process. While nothing can guarantee the failure of a take-over bid, except the rejection of a bid by a majority of shareholders, the presence of socially responsible institutional investors among a company's shareholders will at least mean that one group will listen seriously to (and, one hopes, speak accordingly at any meeting) the view that a long-term and sustainable programme is being followed for long-term value rather than a short-term programme simply to maximize the profit and share value today.

In this book, I have tried to cover a fair amount of ground and, inevitably, there will be some that I have missed. During the time when I was writing, information kept arriving from the various helpful sources that I used and, eventually, I had to draw a line and get on with it. However, the flow of information, which continues to this day, is indicative of the vibrancy of socially responsible and accountable investment as a concept.

When the reader has finished the book, I hope to have explained what ethical, ecological, or socially accountable investment is and what it is not. It is the simple introduction of a previously neglected but valid dimension into the considerations which govern long-term investments; it is not a financial protest movement in which people expect to lose their money for a good cause. If, as a result of reading my words, you come to feel that socially responsible investment is not something out of the mainstream or for other people, then I will be pleased. If you take that one step further and become an ethical or socially responsible investor, then you will be part of the trend which has already made this idea not only a mainstream investment concept but also the fastest growing group investment sector and which ought eventually to make it part of every business's mission to act decently and responsibly.

What I have not set out to do is to advise you what you should do with your own money. First, I cannot know your personal circumstances and second, there are people available to you whose job is just that, advising on what options will be suitable for your requirements in your circumstances.

As far as terminology is concerned, I have tried to distinguish between ethical and environmental or ecological concerns where it matters and have used the more general terms of socially responsible investment and socially accountable business where appropriate. However, the reader should understand that all terms are basically descriptions of investment or business practice with a conscience.

I could never have done the job without help and a good deal of tolerance: help from people in organizations such as the Ethical Investment Research Service (EIRIS), the UK Social Investment Forum (UKSIF), the RSA, Greenpeace and Friends of the Earth, as well as individuals such as Charles Jacob, Roger Morton (both of whom gave generously of their time to offer me the benefits of their vast experience in this arena) and others too numerous to mention; tolerance from my wife, Crena, and my daughter, Camilla, who have had to put up with the odd hours and inconvenient working times that are necessary when writing a book at the same time as one is making a living – in my case, writing articles.

While I have tried to explain and demystify the subject, I lay no claim to originating the philosophy of ethical investment itself. However, it is a philosophy whose sense has become clearer to me as I have been writing.

Part 1

THE PRINCIPLES OF
ETHICAL INVESTMENT

Chapter 1

....

WHY CONCERN YOURSELF?

It is in one of the greatest books ever, the Bible, that an answer can be found to the question posed in the title of this chapter – in the parable of the good Samaritan. An inhuman and immoral act had been committed but people simply ignored its consequences as they passed by on the far side of the road or even crossed the road to avoid any risk of becoming involved in a disaster that had befallen somebody else. It took an individual from beyond the mainstream society in that area at that time to react, not with indifference, nor with the studied ignorance of one who did not wish the flow of his life to be disrupted by an event which, no matter how unpleasant, had not directly occurred to him and certainly not with the deliberate avoidance that has typified reactions to many humanitarian disasters while they were on progress. He reacted instead to some deep and basic human instincts (or so one would hope) of kinship and survival of the species. Kinship because, in tending the victim's wounds, he offered more than mere first aid, he offered his strength, his protection, solidarity, if you like, to stand by a fellow being in a time of distress. Survival of the species because, who knows, if such attacks are random, and they often are, he might himself be the victim on a future occasion. Life is like that. Many events and processes victimize people unable to stand up for themselves or damage the fabric of the world in a way that, while its effects may not be noticeable today, will eventually subtract from rather than add value to life on Earth. At one time, most of us would have asked, 'But what can I do that would have any effect at all on events and processes which are driven by governments or mighty industrial interests or which occur a world away from where I live?'

Who cares? We care

Today, though, things are a little different in that most of us would like to contribute positively to the world but, apart from some very small acts of responsibility or kindness, we may still feel that there is little we can do to shape events or influence the policies and actions of the forces that drive our society. Such modesty would, in most cases, be misplaced. This is a book about a powerful but accessible medium for good through which ordinary people can wield enormous influence while, at the same time, securing their own financial future. About a line of action, open to most people, through which they can have some say in the management of the forces that control the quality as well as the value of their lives and those of millions of others. About a line of action through which they can express their views, pleasure and displeasure more forcibly than at any protest meeting. A line of action which cannot be ignored by those who control the processes which make up our lives.

Most of us would like to contribute positively to the world.

Ordinary people can wield enormous influence while, at the same time, securing their own financial future.

Does anybody care that the atmosphere grows warmer and more polluted by the day? Who will worry that our finely balanced ecosystem which has, over millions of years, created the conditions for life on earth, may be degrading to a point where, within a few years, we can no longer guarantee life-supporting conditions at all times in all places? So what if our comfort is still, on the threshold of the twenty-first century, often bought at the price of human degradation and exploitation, animal suffering or the irreversible despoliation of the planet which we inhabit? Should it concern us that our children may have to content themselves not to see trees or those other Arcadian comforts that help us to soothe away the conditions of a stress-laden lifestyle? The list is long and all too familiar today: it lists the self-defeating short-term benefits at high and damaging long-term financial and moral cost; it also lists the by-products from the processes we employ to create the lifestyle we want – by-products which actually undermine the material or moral fabric of life itself. And yes, we do care or at least enough of us, an increasing number, do care.

In a survey carried out by NOP Research Group for the Ethical Investment Research Society (EIRIS) in 1997 (*see* Figure 1.1) 73 per cent of those polled felt that their pension fund should operate an ethical policy and, within that group, 29 per cent thought that should be the case even if it reduced financial return. That, unfortunately, is an image with which the ethical investment concept is burdened in the eyes of some investors. But if we look a little further into the poll findings, it emerges that twice as many women as men supported this more extreme principle, possibly reflecting a higher level of compassion or perhaps reflecting the comfort of a husband's or partner's pension already able to secure a comfortable retirement. And 44 per cent within the 73 per cent stated that they would favour an ethical scheme only if that criterion does not reduce financial return. Add those to the 19 per cent who want their pension scheme to concentrate on financial returns and ignore ethical factors and it can be seen that, if it is to succeed, ethical investment (including investment which includes ecological concerns within its brief) must stand on its merits as a sound investment philosophy and on that alone. And as we shall see later, there is nowadays no need for ethical investors to take a performance

Figure 1.1
WOULD YOU FAVOUR A PENSION SCHEME THAT . . .

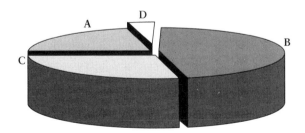

Would you favour a pension scheme that . . .
A concentrates on financial return and ignores ethical factors? 19%
B operates an ethical policy, but only if this does not reduce financial return? 44%
C operates an ethical policy even if it may reduce financial return? 29%
D don't know 8%

shortfall as the price of their principles; not in the short term comparative to similar investments and certainly not in the long term. Indeed, there is no ethical justification for a poor return on money invested, whether that be in the shares of a company or through one of the many collective investment funds available to ordinary investors. Particularly

We ought to be able to make proper provision for our own needs without trampling on the needs and rights of others.

not when the money belongs to savers and investors who have entrusted a fund management team with the security, maintenance and improvement of their savings or inheritance. However, the survey does illustrate an increasing awareness that most of the elements comprising our home planet are finite, that none of them is indestructible and that, given the wealth of late twentieth century society, we ought to be able to make proper provision for our own needs without trampling on the needs and rights of others.

What can we do about it?

So far so good, but then we might wonder what any one of us could do within our lives which would have any practical impact on the larger course of events. Well, quite a lot in reality. Of course, the big events such as the International Earth and Environment Conferences attract a great deal of publicity while they are in progress but usually end with little more than broad global targets and pious intentions to try to do better in future. At worst, they may even end with a market being made in pollution allowances so that the wealthier countries can pollute at will, buying and using the allowances of poorer countries who lack the means to sustain the type of industrial society which might generate their pollution quota! Just such a market opened in Chicago in 1998. The problem for many governments is that they cannot see environmentally responsible policies as vote winners whereas, if the evidence of the past few decades is anything to go by, the fruits of environmental profligacy certainly are proven vote catchers. Also, the events and policies discussed and decided at these stratospherically high-level affairs may seem to have little direct relevance to you or me today.

Many will feel that it is the job of government and intergovernmental bodies to address the international conventions that govern activities from oil extraction to whaling, from animal welfare to child slavery, from nuclear weapons testing to the disposal of nuclear waste. Some do not think so, or at least do not believe that those great and good bodies could be trusted to act on their own initiative without prompting or in the absence of a compelling threat to their own wellbeing. In recent years, organizations such as Greenpeace and Friends of the Earth have risen to prominence as environmental activists. They take matters into their own hands and strike at the perpetrators of what they perceive to be activities harmful to the planet and its environment. Nearer to home, self-styled 'eco-warriors' attend the site of any planned development which will extend the footprint and infrastructure of our resource-hungry economy over any new land. They have become famous for their tree houses, tunnels and Red Indian 'whooping' and have brought to our attention issues and activities that might otherwise have passed unnoticed and unchallenged. This with the result that government plans to extend the road system further have already been drastically curtailed at a saving to the environment and to the Treasury's purse. The question that now has to be asked is, ' If we are not doing all of these things, how will we sustain a tolerable lifestyle, commensurate with the one to which we have grown accustomed?' And then, what can ordinary people, not eco-warriors, not international experts and certainly not politicians, do about it?

Well, we can support the development of processes and organizations which make an effort to produce the artefacts and services to which we have become accustomed in a more ethical and environmentally considerate manner. That is what this book is all about. But there is more. Many of us collect our bottles and newspapers to deposit in the recycling bins at the local supermarket car park while garments that are good enough can be handed in to one of many charity shops which will sell them on to do further service in clothing somebody else at no cost to the environment and little cost to the new owner with the added benefit that whatever proceeds there are will be applied to the promotion of that charitable purpose which the organization seeks to support. Some charities and specific disaster appeals pass the clothing directly to the needy.

We make the effort to insulate our lofts, double-glaze our windows, turn down the thermostat on the central heating, reduce our water consumption and even buy cars whose efficiency will enable us at least to get about at less cost to the environment. Perhaps, if it was a more attractive option, more of us would use public transport or bicycles. But while public transport remains something of a lottery in the thinly populated areas where it may be needed the most, cycling, except as a recreational activity, just is not a practical option for most people in their normal workaday lives. Perhaps, if we knew who they were, more of us would choose to buy from companies whose policy includes the objective of regularly reviewing and seeking to improve the impact of their business on the people and the world around them: companies that considered their workforce, suppliers and customers to be integral and valuable stakeholders in the business – whose workforce was properly paid for working in decent conditions for reasonable hours, whose suppliers were paid a fair price on time for the services and goods supplied and whose customers were sold a serviceable product at a profitable but fair price; companies that took all steps to minimize the effect of their operations on the environment and maximize the quality and efficiency of their processes; companies that included an ethical element in their mission and planning.

Investment with a human dimension

Perhaps what is needed is a means by which we can wield our influence over businesses to act responsibly, target the right businesses at little or no cost to ourselves in money or time and send a financial signal to governments (it is a language that they all understand) that our concerns are real and we are, literally, prepared to put our money where our mouths are. Ethical and environmental investment is that means. More importantly if you plan to invest, it is a fast growing investment sector with a track

The growth of ethical funds has exceeded the overall growth rate of the unit trust sector over the period since 1989.

record (*see* Chapter 9 *Performance: can you afford to put your money where your heart is?*) and strong prospects for the future. Investors can enjoy a return that is decent in every sense of the word and many would if only they knew how.

Research, again by EIRIS and published in August 1997, revealed that, although still a small sector of the group investment market, there has been enormous growth in funds whose managers include ethical, environmental or socially responsible standards and criteria as well as the usual standards of financial probity and potential for profit and growth in their stock selection processes. The growth of ethical funds has exceeded the overall growth rate of the unit trust sector over the period since 1989, as the two charts show (*see* Figures 1.2 and 1.3).

Figure 1.2 shows the growth of ethical funds from the second quarter of 1989 until the second quarter of 1998, during which period ethical funds under management grew from a fraction under £200 million to nearly £2 billion. Perhaps more importantly, that growth has included more than a doubling in value over the three years 1996–8. By the end of 1998, 40 ethical funds had £2 billion under management

Figure 1.2
GROWTH OF ETHICAL UNIT TRUSTS AND ETHICAL INVESTMENT TRUSTS 1989–1998

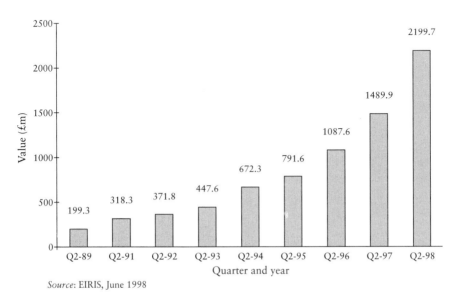

Source: EIRIS, June 1998

and both numbers continue to grow. In practice, total ethical and environmental group investment funds under management passed the £2 billion mark in June 1998 by which time there were 38 funds applying socially responsible criteria to their investment management approach. This figure also represented a 50 per cent increase over the preceding twelve months, so socially responsible investment is no longer a fringe interest but, in growth terms at least, a mainstream investment option. Given that, way back in 1984, original estimates of the market for ethical investments were about £2 million, then to have bettered those estimates by one thousand fold offers a remarkable insight into how our attitudes have changed (even when allowance is made for inflation).

As Figure 1.3 shows, such growth has not been simply the reflection of favourable market conditions. In seven out of the last eight years, ethical unit trusts and ethical investment trusts have grown faster than either all unit trusts and investment trusts or than the market capitalization of the FTSE All-Share index. During the three year period to 1997, total funds under management in unit trusts and investment trusts grew by only 55 per cent while the market capitalization of the FTSE All-Share Index increased by 61 per cent. This has to be viewed in the context of ethical funds at £2.1 billion representing only 1 per cent of total funds in UK unit trusts and investment trusts (January 1999 figures). But that situation reflects another key finding. A large majority of investors and potential investors either are not aware that ethical investment is a possibility open to them or do not know how they could invest at least some of their money in a manner that reflects their feelings as well as their need to generate a fair return.

One example brings home this point very forcefully. In 1997, a pension plan holder selected an ethical fund for her investment. The lady, a designer of websites for companies seeking a presence on the world wide web of the Internet, had only realized that it would be possible to invest in a way that supported her principles when she was designing a website for an insurance company and noticed that part of the content was a small article on animal testing. She read the article because, as a vegetarian and on a general principle, she was against animal testing. The outcome was that she contacted the company and they, in

Figure 1.3

THE GROWTH OF ETHICAL UNIT TRUSTS AND ETHICAL INVESTMENT TRUSTS
COMPARED WITH GROWTH OF ALL UNIT TRUSTS AND INVESTMENT TRUSTS AND GROWTH IN
MARKET CAPITALIZATION OF FTSE ALL-SHARE INDEX

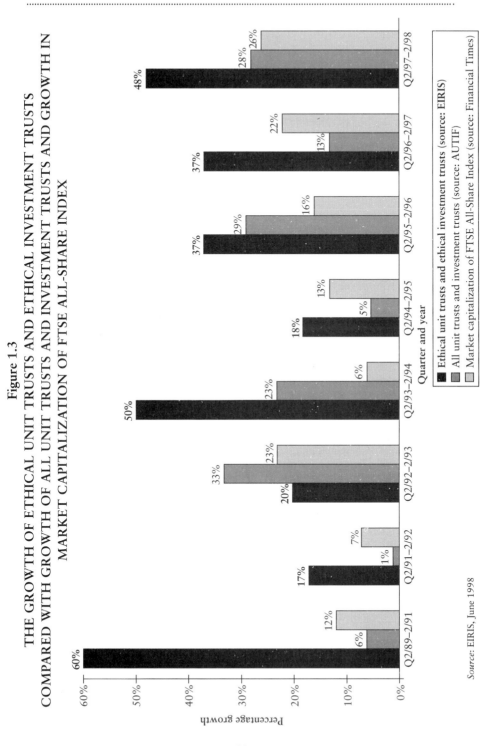

■ Ethical unit trusts and ethical investment trusts (source: EIRIS)
▨ All unit trusts and investment trusts (source: AUTIF)
▨ Market capitalization of FTSE All-Share Index (source: Financial Times)

Source: EIRIS, June 1998

turn, put her in touch with an Independent Financial Adviser (IFA) specializing in offering advice in the ethical sector. Otherwise, she might have established her pension plan without realizing that, as she put it, she could, 'invest my pension in a way that supports my views on life.'

The morning after

We have all, at some time, awoken on a Sunday morning to the steady beat of drums within our head. Hangovers are a familiar but usually an individual experience. However, at the end of the 1980s, it seemed that we were experiencing a collective hangover after a good party at the end of a gruelling week. And it had been a 'gruelling week' from 1945 to 1979 that had ended with the United Kingdom being seen as a 'basket case' with a socialist command economy and suffering from the eponymous 'British Disease', a term used to describe a condition of industrial anarchy, institutional ineptitude and loss of national pride. We needed the 1980s and the rebirth of the United Kingdom into the real world. Had the preceding order been allowed to continue, the ethical and environmental values of investments would, by now, be the least of our concerns as the environmental record of those East European socialist command economies demonstrated. But, as we mature, both individually and collectively, we take more time to reflect and perhaps take life at a less frantic, more indulgent pace than before. Now, there is a wish to avoid the extreme changes that followed the post-war years which means to avoid a similar reaction to the 1980s which would simply restore 'basket case' Britain. Part of the present government's appeal was a sense that they promised to seek a more sensible middle way. Many people have gained from their incomes, pension funds, privatization shares and windfalls accumulated during the Thatcher years and many have gained through inheritance from the post-war home-owning boom. They naturally wish to preserve the value of that wealth but there is also a sense that, if those who have gained continue to exclude any consideration of those who have been less fortunate, then the natural ebb and flow of society will eventually threaten that wealth. Equally, if that money is invested for the highest immediate return regardless of the long-term cost of those activities in which an investment is made, then there is a sense that we may be securing our excessive comfort today by pillaging the very staples of life from future generations. Yet, through that wealth, for the first time ever, a majority of the population have the means to apply not political but economic pressure to those points in the system where they would like to see change – in particular, where they would like to see implemented the kind of forward-thinking policies with respect to people and the environment that will not take today's comforts at the expense of tomorrow's quality of life for all. Because most individual wealth is nowadays held in the group investment funds which underpin pensions, life insurance, unit trusts and so on, if a group of people who share a particular set of standards and values all invest with a fund which also shares those standards and values, they can become a significant force to apply the economic pressure required. Economic pressure does not engender the same passions as political pressure or protest movements but it does bring about change and that is what really matters.

We may be securing our excessive comfort today by pillaging the very staples of life from future generations.

Economic pressure does bring about change and that is what really matters.

For all the practical and sensible reasons set out above, we should not forget that the underlying reason why people concern themselves is not one of economics or politics or a wish to be difficult but one of care. When Friends Provident, whose Stewardship Fund is the longest established UK fund with ethical, environmental and socially responsible criteria built in to its investment model, conducted its third annual survey, 31 per cent of respondents agreed that their principal reason for choosing the Stewardship Fund was that the investment criteria reflected their own concerns. One respondent, when asked to sum up their view, explained, 'Money talks, but at least mine says, "let's be nice to one another".'

So the reasons why we should concern ourselves are many but the bottom line may be because, for this generation more than any who have gone before, we can do something about turning our principles into the standards and priorities of the organizations that count — those that require money, our money, to continue building their business. And at the same time, we can make an investment that will earn us returns from sustainable activities which ought to be as capable of delivering a return in ten years as they are today.

Chapter 2

THE ADVANTAGES OF ETHICAL INVESTMENT

Sacrifice? No, thank you!

There is something in our human psyche which conditions us to assume that, if what we are doing is good, then it must be at some sacrifice to our own best interests. Phrases such as 'doing the right thing' and 'taking advantage' express in a few words our whole hang-up concerning how we feel about the cost of acting correctly and the ethics of looking after our own best interests. And it's all rubbish, absolute rubbish. With the possible exception of acts of individual bravery, we do what we perceive as beneficial to ourselves. When calculating the benefit of our actions for ourselves or others, we can make two cardinal mistakes.

The first mistake would be always to value that benefit in monetary terms because some people get their sense of well-being from feeling that they have added something to the sum value of human life and some, it must be said, bask in the glory of their 'sacrifice'. The second mistake would be to ignore the tribal or species element in our psyche. We do not always act from individual motivations but may often act as the one member of the human race, or our tribe in it, able to do something right now.

So our self-interest may grow from different motivations at different times but we save and invest money in order to achieve a return and some growth. The specific purpose is usually so that the accumulated savings or investment will be able to do a job for us in the future such as redeem a mortgage, realize a long-cherished dream or provide for our increasing material needs in retirement and, perhaps, enable us to take that step earlier than might have ordinarily been the case. Given that, there is no sense in placing our money where it will be at any disadvantage or where its performance will cost us any sacrifice, not simply of the money itself but particularly of the purpose for which we are saving or investing it. Unfortunately, socially accountable investment (whether ethically or environmentally motivated or both) has, in the past, carried that aura of sacrifice which may go a long way towards explaining why, until recently, it remained a little visited corner of the investment market. Equally, it may be the dawning realization that short-term gains are sometimes at the expense of long-term benefits that has begun to raise interest in the sector and seen more investors and, significantly, more fund managers explore the opportunity to think that way. Certainly, the improving performance of the sector as it matures will have influenced a number of people to look further into socially accountable investment. Much of the credit must go to pioneers such as Friends Provident, whose Stewardship Fund set the ball rolling, and to organizations such as EIRIS (the Ethical Investment Research Service) and UKSIF (the UK Social Investment Forum) who have made available the information needed to achieve understanding but do not discount self-interest as a perfectly good reason why investors should consider a socially responsible investment. There are many advantages in investing ethically and some of those advantages are financial.

Short-term gains are sometimes at the expense of long-term benefits.

There are many advantages in investing ethically and some of those advantages are financial.

You can make a difference

In one company's office, among the certificates and management buzz words on the wall behind the boss's desk, there hangs a framed motto which simply reads, 'The goldsmith's rule: He who has the gold makes the rules.' The love of money may well be at the root of all evil although possibly power, lust and pious incompetence may actually account for more of that condition, but money is also a significant engine for good and money certainly does talk. Indeed, it would be hard to imagine a human activity in which money (or the barter of goods and services) does not play a part nowadays. Communism was the only system which ever seriously advanced the notion that money was not required within a society but the system never lived up to its pious aspirations and ultimately paid the price of flying in the face of human nature. Any remaining outposts of the communist system which may still exist will be conspicuous by their failure to meet even the most basic human aspirations. Capitalism rules, OK! And in the capitalist system, the goldsmith's rule holds good.

Companies require capital in order to establish and equip their operation and, to raise that money beyond the pocket of the founder or the inclination of the bank manager, they issue shares in the business. Those shares in the business are purchased by individuals or institutions with capital to invest and capital is money. Capitalism relies on market forces: where people and institutions believe they can get the best value for their capital, to attract money to successful operations and deny it to failing ones. That is an over-simplification but crudely sums up the way the system works. Of course, once a company's shares have been initially issued and bought, the price which people are prepared to pay for them in future trading neither puts money into nor takes money from the business – not directly, at least. However, whether or not investors are prepared to buy the shares of a company reflects their calculation of the likely value of those shares in projected income and growth terms. So, if investors believe that the company has good prospects, they will wish to buy its shares and that will push up the price of those shares whereas, if they feel that the prospects for the business are not so good, they will not wish to buy and may even wish to sell any shares that they do hold which will push down the share price. If the share price is high and/or rising, the company will have no trouble raising short-term capital (borrowing) or long-term capital (further issues of shares) to fund developments. On the other hand, a company whose share price is low and/or falling will find either that the bank is reluctant to help in the short term or that the price of that help is too high while new share issues will either not be taken up or have to be sold at a discount to face value. Also, if the share price is low, competitors may be encouraged to make take-over bids. The system works because it tends to support the survival of the fittest in the long term. In this climate, and it is the one which has prevailed across most of the world, companies take decisions and structure their operations in a way that will ensure the share price stays high and rising.

Ethical and ecological investors can exploit this system to introduce their particular value system into the equation with a result that will be more powerfully effective in the long term than any number of protests. Traditionally, the way for companies to achieve high share valuations and thus, by implication, a high rating of the management team's competence and future prospects, has been to focus on the profit and the dividend which can be paid to shareholders in the short term. And the reason for that is because investors have always seemed to value short-term profit. But there has also been a longer-term consideration by which investors also expect growth in the value of their investment. However, that again has often been linked in investors' minds to an expectation that profits will continue to be high. Where ethical or socially accountable investment makes a difference is that investors do not simply look to this year's profit as a measure of how well the business is doing; they also weigh into the equation the performance and activities of the business in broader terms. So, even if the profit is high this year, if that has been earned wholly or in part from unethical activities – by reducing the value in a non-renewable resource, by making the cheapest rather than the best arrangements for disposing of waste, by poor treatment of employees or any other of the criteria by which socially responsible business practice is judged – socially aware investors who consider the whole picture will not wish to buy the company's shares. If enough investors take that view, then part of what management teams set out to achieve will be to operate in a manner which ensures that the company's shares are wanted by socially responsible investors.

And we must not forget that the boards of directors who run companies have to face their shareholders each year at the annual general meeting to explain their actions in the past year and answer questions. Either as individual shareholders or, more likely, through the fund managers who control collective investments, socially responsible investors can raise the topics which relate to the long-term costs of any short-term gains and whether the broader implications of any policy have been considered or whether their implications are included in the strategy to implement that policy. In these ways, by influencing the price of shares with their support or otherwise and by raising issues of real concern at shareholders' meetings, socially concerned investors can make a difference to the priorities and activities of modern business.

Socially concerned investors can make a difference to the priorities and activities of modern business.

But more importantly, they can make a difference to the share price, if the findings of a 1997 North American study of share price movements are correct. In the November/December 1997 issue of the *Ethical Investor*, the newsletter of EIRIS, it was reported that academics Robert D Klassen from Western Ontario and Curtis P McLaughlin from North Carolina had argued that winning an environmental award tends to boost the price of a company's shares by 0.82 per cent while oil spills or other environmental disasters will be followed by a 1.5 per cent fall in the share price. Other studies in the US have also reached the conclusion that announcements of ethical failings can cause the share price of the corporation in question to fall by as much as 2.3 per cent. Klassen's and McLaughlin's findings, which were initially published in the journal *Management Science*, suggest that the losses on share value exceed the cost of cleaning up after a disaster although, of course, the lost share value does not come out of the company's coffers but it does have the kinds of effects set out above. At the time when the findings of the Klassen McLaughlin study were published, EIRIS executive director Peter Webster said; 'They suggest that the market is assuming there will be lots of other effects, apart from cleaning up the mess, but it may be that the market is showing the influence that ethical investors are having as well.'

At the Kyoto earth summit in 1997, former UK Minister for the Environment, John Gummer, told delegates that BP's share price had risen following the company's withdrawal from the Global Climate Coalition group of oil companies campaigning against an effective agreement on greenhouse gas emissions. Shell followed BP out of the coalition, a signal, if ever there was one, that large companies can certainly see the disadvantages of not listening to ethical investors and may even be seeing the advantages of listening.

Knowledge is strength

Because of the high profile and extensive publicity given to lottery and competition winners today, we often forget that most success is born of knowledge and, even more importantly, the diligent application of that knowledge rather than luck, although even the most successful investor or fund manager would not be so arrogant as to exclude some contribution from luck in his or her success. This truth extends through life. It is true for the shopkeeper who monitors sales of all lines in order to arrange the display so that, to reach the popular lines, shoppers must pass the rest of the stock or who holds prices on the lines that sell well while loudly cutting prices on less popular lines. It is equally true for the politician who commissions research to find out what concerns the voters and then promulgates that concern as a key priority. And it is certainly true of the investment fund manager.

Successful fund managers use a technique of asset allocation and stock selection to identify companies, investment in which will meet the objectives that the fund has set for itself within the criteria that define it. Thus, if a fund is described as 'Far East Growth' shares will need to be in Far Eastern businesses whose share price looks undervalued in the long term or whose plans are considered likely to deliver an expansion of the business and therefore achieve growth. On the other hand, a 'UK Income' fund will seek shares in UK companies which are expected to return good profits and therefore pay good dividends in the future. This investment method works. Almost all investment fund managers who perform consistently well will cite their asset allocation and stock selection procedures as the grounds for their success. And how do these procedures work? Well, behind every successful fund manager there sits an investment analyst who in turn is backed up by a team of researchers.

In the first place, the asset allocation is not simply a matter of listing all of the shares in a particular region or sector. After all, within the Far

East, say, there are many economies whose performances, although linked as are all world economies, are at different stages in the economic cycle, who have different strengths and weaknesses and who are, perhaps, constrained by different regulations, financial controls or workplace attitudes. Equally, within a particular sector, say, energy, there will be extraction and delivery systems, even products that are on the ascendant or are facing a barrage of disapproval which, if translated into legislation in the key economies, might affect the share performance of companies whose interests are committed to particular systems or products.

At the level of individual investments, the detailed research is even more important, for while the broad sweep of information about a region or sector will be reported daily by the press and major investment analysis groups, individual company outlooks which are right for some investors will be wrong for others. If you were looking for income, a business with high growth prospects would not be the right one for your objectives even though it may well be an intrinsically sound investment. So the research which supports stock selection must investigate a number of issues. It is important to know the past record of the business and what trends might be discerned from that record. The fund manager will need to consider whether that record suggests the stock will meet the criteria set for the fund or whether the trend of results, if it continues, will meet those criteria. But, of course, investment success cannot be left to chance and so, even if the company's past record is in line with what the fund is seeking, there will need to be evidence that the management team has not neglected any area in the business which might create later problems and has plans in place to ensure control of events and outcomes in the future. There will also need to be evidence that there are no financial or other issues in subsidiary, parent or associate businesses which might later impact upon the proposed investment. This is very important because fund managers generally like to pick an investment then stick with it to reap the reward of their own far-sightedness rather than chop and change their holdings. That would be costly because every investment, whether a success or not, starts out using the same amount of research resource and share dealing costs are the same for good buys or bad.

But it is not enough to have plans. Fund managers will wish to be sure that the business has the resources – both human and financial as well as material and systems – to carry through those plans which otherwise may be no more than fond hopes. For instance, where change is planned, investing fund managers will want to know that the training is arranged to ensure that personnel are able to get the best value out of the new situation and that the plans include the necessary actions to meet any legislative or market requirements. Then, given all of the above information together with some intuition and 'local' knowledge, a fund manager can put a value on the prospects for the business in terms which would meet the wishes of his or her investors.

A fund manager can put a value on the prospects for the business in terms which would meet the wishes of his or her investors.

That would be the requirement for any fund manager operating in the equity markets. However, for the manager of an ethical or ecological fund, there needs to be a further raft of information. He or she will need to know whether the business is involved in any products, services or trade which fall outside the ethical or ecological criteria set for the fund. The way in which the business is run with regard to its main stakeholder groups will also need to be well understood and documented. It will be important to know whether the business is likely to face any financial or legislative pressure which might cast a doubt on its ability to continue to operate within the ethical or ecological criteria of the fund.

But companies do not operate in isolation and so the research must include some very detailed consideration of the businesses of any subsidiary, parent or associate businesses, not just as to potential financial or litigation problems but also as to what they produce and how they measure up to the socially accountable standards of the fund. There will also be a need to check the conditions under which components are manufactured and the use to which the product is applied after sale. Information technology (IT) companies find this a particularly difficult issue as, while by and large their businesses are clean, sometimes their products are put to military or other repressive purposes. It all means that a great deal of research is needed to be sure that the potential investment is a business that, as far as is humanly possible, operates to socially responsible standards and is pre- pared to be socially accountable for its actions. Even if it is, ethical and ecolog- ical fund managers will then apply exactly the same stringent financial cri- teria to a potential investment as any other fund manager because nobody would regard poor management of other people's money as ethical.

Research is needed to be sure that the potential investment is a business that, as far as is humanly possible, operates to socially responsible standards.

Much of this type of research is conducted by EIRIS and many fund managers take advantage of that organization's independent resources to understand the true situation in respect of a potential investment. All in all, ethical and ecological fund managers use more research than others and while the additional resources used may vary, estimates of 40 per cent more are not uncommon. Also, because, in the nature of socially responsible criteria, not all businesses will even get onto the list of potential investments, ethical and ecological fund managers usually work within a smaller group of companies. It all adds up to the fact that ethical and ecological fund mangers will know their investments better than most and that additional knowledge translates into greater investment strength.

In tune with the times

Strip away all the hype, puffed up self-importance at various confer- ences and political vote trawling; grandstanding is grandstanding whatever the cause. Look past the litter often inflicted on the environ- ment by self-styled ecological campaigners; the means may be careless but the cause is not. Reject the cruelty inflicted on wild animals when farmed mink (one of nature's most voracious predators) are released into the wild; a stupid protest does not mean that there is nothing to protest about. Even, if you wish, dismiss protesters as anarchists look- ing for any opportunity to engage the resources of the state; many good causes are hijacked and distorted towards other ends. However, think what you will about the methods employed by some activists to draw our attention to particular matters, there can be no more sense in destroying the environmental balance on which we depend than in sawing off a tree branch on which we are sitting. And there can be no sense in treating people so badly that they ultimately look for deliverance to systems far more hostile than an investor with an ethical agenda. Just being pragmatic, it is dawning on most people that we need to change the way in which we run our system in order to be fairer to a broader group of people and for our processes to add value rather than simply mortgaging future value in order to live well today. It is called sustainable development and socially responsible investment fund managers look for it as a sign of far-sighted management. Whereas perhaps, in the 1980s, socially accountable investment held little appeal for people who believed that they were on a fast track to perpetual prosperity, the philosophy of decency and intelligent custodianship of resources is in tune with thinking in the last years of the twentieth and first years of the twenty-first centuries.

The facts, if nothing else, have driven a change in attitudes. In a 1998 British Chambers of Commerce and Alex Lawrie survey of 3,735 businesses (all sizes, all sectors) over half, 55 per cent, of those surveyed had suffered increased costs and 30 per cent had lost business as a result of road congestion. The survey also found that, 'businesses are concerned about the effects of congestion on the environment and are taking action to combat the problem – including staggering staff times and changing the frequency and time of deliveries.' The awareness is there and an understanding that investors who support the long-term strategy that usually goes with a 'green' agenda will actually help strengthen the arm of those managers who would rather do the right thing. Ethical investors can provide a valuable window on the world for management teams who would benefit from stepping back and seeing the full context in which their business operates.

Ethical investors can provide a valuable window on the world for management teams.

Companies which look to their ethical and ecological responsibilities are generally well managed companies. Just as fund managers need more information to understand companies in this group, so the management teams of those companies need to look properly at their business and, in so doing, will become aware of more than just ethical and ecological matters. For instance, if a business looks carefully at the way in which its waste is disposed of, it may turn out that toxic or non-degradable waste is being dumped in a manner that could potentially harm the environment and any people who come in contact with it. While the immediate issue may not be serious, managers might well conclude that future legislation could outlaw that particular disposal process and may even face the business with the cost of dismantling the dump and restoring it to a natural state or of compensating anyone who may have been harmed by the materials that have been dumped. So it could well be financially as well as environmentally sensible to address the issue now when it is within the control of the company to decide what to do and the timescale in which to do it. That would be preferable to waiting until forced to do something in a timescale determined by someone else with little or no consideration of whether that suits the business or not. But a further bonus might be that, in seeking a better way to dispose of waste, the company may move to recycling waste as a useful material for another process or incineration in a plant which will meet its own costs and might even make a profit from energy production.

Treating workers well, as companies as large as BT have discovered, means that ideas for improvement to the process often come up from the workplace. Also, lower staff turnover means that training costs are lower, because fewer people need to go through the process, and then additional training becomes viable which, in turn, will improve the running of the business still further. Treating suppliers and customers fairly means that the quality of inputs can more easily be controlled in the context of a long established and mutually beneficial supplier/client relationship: similarly, cus-

Companies working with an ethical and ecological component to their mission are companies in tune with the future.

tomer loyalty takes some of the negative pressure away from the marketing effort so that, instead of working to overcome poor perceptions, the business can work to develop positive perceptions and grow its place in the market. All of this can be translated as quality and efficiency which in turn mean more money to pay the workforce a fair return for their input and more money to reward shareholders for the use of their capital. Companies working with an ethical and ecological component to their mission are companies in tune with the future and unlikely to be caught expensively on the hop by future changes in the requirements of society or by changes dictated by common sense.

At the John Reynolds lecture in 1997, Terry Thomas, managing director of the Co-operative Bank, said: 'What shareholders or members want cannot be summed up in a simplistic statement "to enhance shareholder value", since it ignores the issues surrounding how to increase shareholder value across time, not just by the next reporting period.' That is the key: investors who wish to make a profit and those who wish to do the right thing need not have conflicting priorities. From the group who participated in the EIRIS survey (*see* Chapter 1) all three main groups identified can meet their aspirations and gain from the advantages of an ethical investment environment.

Bring it on home

For most people, their largest investment is the property in which they live but, equally, a significant proportion of the pollution we cause is the result of generating more power than we really need in order to cater for the energy inefficiency of our homes. Norwich and Peterborough Building Society (N&P) has addressed this issue from a different angle. To encourage developers to build energy-efficient houses, N&P now offers a 'green' mortgage on which borrowers benefit (at the time of writing) from a 2 per cent discount off the society's standard variable mortgage rate for two years plus other benefits – all available when purchasing properties with a Standard Assessment Procedures (SAP) energy efficiency rating of 80 or more. The higher the rating, the more efficient the property.

There ought to be a law about it!

Most usually, society expresses its requirements as laws and there are a number of legislative programmes rolling forward that will cause expensive problems for businesses which have ignored their social responsibilities. Conversely, businesses that have acknowledged and addressed those issues will find themselves at an advantage. We cannot predict what laws will be enacted in various countries over the next few years but there are some obvious examples of the type of thing we might expect from the international, European and United Kingdom perspectives.

In the first place, the earth summits of recent years may not have changed much but they have begun to change attitudes by publicizing the issues that will impinge on the ecological balance that preserves not just life as we know it but life entire. The limits that have been placed on emissions may well owe much to the poker skills and negotiating powers of the various delegates but the fact that polluting emission limits have been quantified at all is a step forward which acknowledges that things cannot carry on as they are. Of course, there is now a market in which countries can trade their emission allowances so that large industrial economies can continue to pollute using the allowances of smaller, less industrialized nations. But that does not change the fact that there is an overall target for emission levels. Far-sighted companies will start now to prepare for real reductions in the levels that are allowed either following the summit to negotiate the next group of reductions or, perhaps, following some environmental disaster on a scale that may dwarf the forest fires pollution that has covered large areas of South East Asia in recent years. Where would it be best to invest? In a company that ignores all of these warnings, makes no effort to plan and implement cumulative measures to reduce its levels of polluting emissions steadily but consistently and will arrive at any major legislative event unprepared and needing to divert enormous resources to resolve the problem? Or would it be better to invest in a business which makes tackling the issue an integral part of quality management in the organization so that, come any major legislation requirements, the company will be able to continue with business as usual, delivering its normal product or service along with continuing improvements in its environmental performance?

In Europe there are a number of environmental and ethical areas in which the law is taking a stand. Water quality is a case in point where very strict standards for the purity and potability of water have been established which the water businesses are meeting with steady but quite high levels of investment. Also in Europe, there is a growing body of employment legislation which places on businesses the onus to work within the parameters of decent incomes for employees, reasonable holiday times, good standards of health and safety and equality of treatment regardless of race, sex or creed. For businesses that have

In Europe there are a number of environmental and ethical areas in which the law is taking a stand.

always paid regard to these matters, the new legislation may mean little more than tweaking already sound systems to match the specific framing of the legislation. However, for those who have made no effort in this direction, compliance with the legislation may well require a major programme of rapid development with the costs concentrated over a short period of time and resources diverted from the usual purposes of the business. It is often during such management crisis that market share and valued customers are lost so ignoring the trend towards more decent business practices may prove costly.

On the UK front, a simple piece of legislation such as the Late Payment Act will cause no problems for businesses that already pay suppliers in good time but those who have habitually held payments back for one, two or even three months past the normally accepted 30-day payment period will have suddenly found that they must meet all payments in time and will have had to catch up two or three months' bills all at once which could well prove a strain on cashflow.

As regards the future legislative moves towards a better environment and more decent standards of business conduct, it would not take a genius to see the way the world is going and what it might cost those who try to swim against that tide. (The issue of legislation and its effect on business practice is examined further in Chapter 10.)

I feel good!

This chapter has tried to set out some of the financial and business advantages for ethical and ecological investment but it would be remiss not to give space to the emotional advantages of doing the right thing. No matter how much people may be moved by issues related to ethics and the environment, with the exception of a few activists and committed people, they will not be prepared to risk their savings, their family's security and their retirement on an emotionally strong but financially uncertain proposition. And this is quite understandable. But if you can see the sense of socially responsible business practice as simply being good business practice, then it is also good to realize that, in committing the voice of your money to that system, you may well be adding pressure to help today. You will be help-

> *In committing the voice of your money, you may well be adding pressure to help.*

ing to create a business community in which today's added value is generated from skills applied in a quality workplace rather than from raiding the future and depleting at an unsustainable rate those resources that our children and grandchildren will need in order to enjoy their time on earth as much as we enjoy ours. And if that makes you feel good, good!

The bottom line

Ethically and ecologically based investment is not a sacrifice of your present well-being for some ill-defined future good. It is an investment made for all the reasons that one ever makes an investment with the added clear understanding that, in a world of finite resources and where communications are so efficient that, sooner or later, everybody will know if a company treats people badly or depletes finite resources for short-term profit, doing the right thing is not only morally good but is also good business for everybody.

Chapter 3

THE DIFFERENT 'GREEN' CREDENTIALS AND CONCERNS THAT MOTIVATE PEOPLE

With the possible exception of identical twins, no two people are identical and no two people hold identical sets of values. We can certainly agree on the broad sweep of our beliefs and largely agree on the detail of opinion with a significant part of the population but our own beliefs are moulded by the forces that make us and, in that, genetics are only one factor. Our family circumstances and experiences, the conditions in which we were brought up and live now, that family's and our own relative station in society, what has happened to us or those about whom we care and our perception of the degree to which our actions and views

Our own beliefs are moulded by the forces that make us.

might have any impact on the world at large – all of these things and more help to determine the things in which we believe, our own preferred direction for the future of society, the people in it and the activities in which it engages. There is a simple term to describe the rich variety of beliefs, circumstances and demeanours to be found around us: it is called 'human nature' and provides the colour, the depth, the inspiration and the structures which make life – for better or for worse.

Just as we all are unique in other respects, so we each hold slightly varying views on what environmental issues are worthy of concern, what are ethical practices and what priorities should govern the conduct of corporate organizations. It is worth spending a little time setting out the possible views that we might hold so that we may more easily understand and be able to express our own concerns and motivations with regard to socially accountable, ethical or environmental issues. Then we can start to decide in what areas we would like our own savings and investments to be influential and what we might want that influence to achieve.

Specific priorities

Friends Provident, who launched the first Stewardship Fund, conduct a bi-annual survey among the fund's investors to gauge their priorities for socially responsible investment criteria. The top three positive criteria were:

1 conservation of energy and of natural resources
2 environmental improvements and pollution control
3 providing high quality products and services which are of long-term benefit to the community

while the top three negative criteria were:

1 environmental destruction
2 exploitation of third world countries
3 trade with oppressive regimes.

However, those are the views of people who have considered this matter for some time and are already committed ethical investors. How, though, will those who are still considering this investment alternative be able to crystallize their own concerns?

The environment

Ask any school student what they think should be the first five priorities of government and a majority will trot out a list including, 'the en-viron-ment'. The problem is that, although they all know the term by rote, the litter that often remains after a large group of school-age young people have moved on suggests that they have a less firm grasp on the full meaning of the issue. In truth, most people's understanding of this complex and vital component in life is limited to the focus of campaigns that hit the headlines and lasts for about as long as they are on the front page. But that should not lead us to diminish the importance of the physical world, the forces which continue to shape it and the fine balances that have led to the presence and continuance of life on this planet. And it should certainly not lead us into taking all that for granted or becoming complacent about the very real concerns that are becoming increasingly apparent for the condition and future of our environment. Inevitably, our activities, what we take from and put into that physical balance can enhance or reduce the degree to which the whole natural structure is able to support life as we know it. As far as activities on a small scale are concerned, we can each add our own little common sense contribution to daily life: recycling paper and bottles, conserving water, insulating our homes, avoiding unnecessary energy consumption; all of these are within our personal remit and all are important but are not

We can each add our own little common sense contribution to daily life.

really subjects for this book. On the other hand, activities on a large scale are usually conducted by governments and corporate organizations so that it is easy to believe (as cynics might say we are intended to believe) that such global matters should be left to those in charge. However, 'those in charge' are there on our sufferance and are no less human than the rest of us. In fact, a brief look at the newspapers might lead you to believe that people who seek power are more prone to human weakness than the rest of us and that the power only makes things worse. As the old saying puts it, 'power corrupts and absolute power corrupts absolutely.' In most countries today we do have a means to change our governments every few years and so can express our concerns on their

At annual general meetings, the power of the ballot is at hand.

environmental performance at that time and through our political representatives in government at other times. However, until recently it has been true that most people have felt powerless in the face of large corporations where we cannot so obviously wield the power of the ballot that we can wield over politicians. But, with the arrival of socially accountable investment, a means is now to hand through which ordinary people can express their views on corporate behaviour in the language which most organizations understand: money and investment. And, at annual general meetings, the power of the ballot is at hand.

Elementary, my dear investor

The concept of the environment is not new. For many centuries before science became as precise as it is today, the world was believed to be comprized of the elements Earth, Air, Fire and Water. It was the presence and balance of these elements that was believed to hold the key to life, while an excess of any one could lead to disaster. Not much has changed. The environment still consists of Earth, Air and Water while, if we consider Fire to be the processes by which we fashion those 'elements' into the material components of life on earth . . . Well, there you are, not much has changed.

The earth itself has provided all of the ingredients for our life today. Everything around us is made from materials either that the earth produced as crops of one sort or another or that have been extracted from the earth itself. But that is where the problems arise. Sometimes, the ways in which we maximize the productivity of crops or the processes by which we extract material from the earth, can lead to damage or waste deposits which have the potential to upset that balance on which life (and not only human life) depends. Environmentally concerned investors who believe that the maintenance of that balance may best be achieved through restraint of current methods of extraction and cropping try to avoid making their money available to businesses involved in those activities.

However, some would say that it is more practical to find alternatives to current methods and they might well be prepared to invest in an enterprise that produces food organically, by permaculture methods or by using other low impact systems that seek to harness the natural order rather than fight it. Others might wish to consider the impact on jobs, livelihoods and the cohesion of communities that any sudden change could bring about. They might prefer to make their money available subject to some assurance that the company was endeavouring to clean up its act, not only with fine words but with a verifiable programme of development.

Others still would prefer to invest in businesses engaged in positive activities to restore and maintain a balance in the earth – reclaiming quarries and open-cast mines, re-establishing habitats and generally restoring land to its original state, or as near as is practically possible – or managing the disposal of waste with the least impact on the balance of the environment.

In my water

Water, because of its make-up as a liquid, can be used as part of many processes, particularly as a cooling medium for processes that produce heat and as a cleaning or carrier medium which can quickly and cheaply remove unwanted chemicals and by-products from the site of a process. The problem is that, in performing those tasks, the water itself becomes different and its ability to sustain life which is often at the lower end of a long food chain is threatened. Also, because of its ability to produce energy through hydro-electric systems and its value as part of the agricultural cycle on land, water is a much prized resource. For this reason, it is often hoarded and even appropriated by companies and countries to the detriment of their neighbours and communities around about.

Those concerned with the quality of the environment would often prefer not to invest in companies whose activities might pollute, mis-appropriate or hoard water to the detriment of its ability to sustain life or to the detriment of others who need to use it. On the other hand, some might see it as sensible to direct their money at companies whose activities, while fundamentally damaging, are carefully managed to minimize that damage and, wherever the damage occurs, to take planned steps aimed at restoring the balance. If that can be done by re-using the pollutant and thus avoiding yet another process, so much the better. This is more often possible where water used to cool one process can be used to provide heat elsewhere and thus both restore its own condition and provide heat where it is required at minimal cost. Others again might prefer to invest in companies who seek out alter-natives to the use of water in the ways in which it is currently used. Given the current outlook for climate change, this might prove a prof-itable as well as balanced policy.

Hot air

Perhaps the sub-title should be 'the air that I breathe' because both the heat and the composition of our air are cause for grave, and probably the most immediate, concern. Air is possibly the most fragile element in the environment and can be all too easily mistreated because, except in the immediate vicinity of a pollution source, it does not obviously show when it has been damaged. Nevertheless, since the industrial revolution began, a steady stream of polluting gases have gradually overwhelmed the ability of the air over the industrialized parts of the world to restore its own balance naturally. The resulting changes to the composition of air are showing themselves in a number of ways. Incidences of asthma and other pollution-related conditions are increasing although there is still dispute over the extent to which air pollution can contribute to some of the conditions with which it has been associated. However, nobody would deny the fact that polluted air cannot be good for organisms, including ourselves, which evolved over millions of years in clean air and which, according to the worst prognosis, must now adapt to or put up with polluted air (because the change has been too fast for evolution). The other great problem is that, as we add increasing levels of often caustic chemicals to the air, its natural self-restorative powers are lost, with the result that some of the atmospheric features necessary to life have begun to break down. Most notably, damage to the ozone layer, which protects the lower atmosphere and the earth itself from harmful solar radiation, is regarded as the prime contributor to the phenomenon of global warming which, in turn, is causing polar ice to melt, sea levels to rise and areas that once had damp temperate climates to veer between extreme cold wet and hot dry conditions.

Investors who are concerned might well wish to avoid those companies who use the air as a cheap, convenient way of exhausting their pollution or companies whose products will eventually add unnatural and unbalancing chemicals into the delicate balance of the atmosphere. As before, others may consider the effects on employment and communities of too rapid a change in practice and others still might actively support companies who are seeking or operating systems and processes that contain and treat the dangerous emissions.

Think right, do right, be right

Whichever aspect of the environment we are considering, investors who want to make a difference need to seek investment funds whose managers will look for particular traits in the behaviour of businesses towards the environment.

In the first instance, those who promote the cause of a balanced and healthy environment believe that businesses must start to look longer term in their planning and decision processes. It is perfectly possible to take a decision that will maximize profits this year while building up trouble for future times. Indeed, there have been examples where businesses have neglected well documented evidence of harbingers of trouble in order to maximize the return for today's shareholders. This actually creates a situation that would be very costly for future shareholders who then find themselves retroactively subsidising the poor practices of earlier times. And that is taking no account of the social cost of such policies.

For instance, a number of businesses concerned with asbestos found themselves in a situation where profits in the fifties and sixties were, to some extent, bought at the expense of environmental and financial costs which came home to roost in the seventies and eighties. Now, the main reason why companies take a short-term bottom-line approach is shareholder pressure and so the enlightened approach of environmentally aware investors and fund managers, expressed as investment policy, should aim to motivate management teams to think longer term.

Wherever possible, lower impact processes are better for the environment and companies who employ or develop such processes are often the ones in tune with the environmental times. But, just as importantly, low-impact processes are often cheaper to run than their high-impact equivalents and rather than using up the resources they need, can work from renewable or sustainable resources. For instance, a windmill power generator will have a lower impact on the environment than a coal-fired power generator, even taking account of the visual impact and the noise, and requires no permanent manning nor anything like the maintenance. Equally, by designing equipment to operate at higher temperatures, cooling systems can be reduced or eliminated which means lower environmental impact from chemicals such as CFCs and lower costs. One excellent example is modern aircraft engines which make more efficient use of fuel and so create less environmental damage, are quieter than the previous generation of aircraft and cost less to run. That said, aircraft engines could not be considered environmentally friendly.

However, sometimes, it has to be admitted, a process which is fundamental to our lifestyle and quality of life cannot avoid environmental damage. With the growth of separated and single parent families, we need to build homes to house an ever growing population who occupy ever more households. The material with which those houses are built is largely quarried from the ground and the workings do leave horrible scars on the landscape. Where physical impact cannot be avoided, concerned investors should be looking for companies who, after they have completed their work, make an effort to restore the environment to the condition in which they had found it or who undertake that work on behalf of others.

Where even restoration is impractical (you could hardly restore an aluminium can to the original ore from which the metal was smelted or a plastic drinks bottle to the petrochemical ingredient from which the plastic was made), then a concerned approach might look to invest in businesses who have found ways to recycle waste products as raw materials for another process (such as the playground flooring made from finely chopped old tyres) or as fuel (there are a number of waste incinerators that now contribute power to the national grid).

The environment is a key issue for many concerned investors and, through a better understanding of what it is, how it works and what steps might be taken to keep the damage that the human race does within the environment's capacity to repair and restore itself, we can begin to focus on what environmental concerns motivate us.

The environment is a key issue for many concerned investors.

Clear, honest and decent

The term with which most people would be familiar is the definition used by the advertising standards authority, 'legal, honest and decent', to describe a fair advertisement. However, legality is a strictly limited term and may not accord with everybody's idea of what is right. It is a word sometimes appropriated by those who wish to put up a defensive position for a morally equivocal activity. And there are plenty of examples in recent history of words being legally misappropriated by people and institutions whose purposes and actions were more or less the opposite of what most of us would understand the words to mean and where use of a particular word made matters anything but clear. Nations that include 'democratic' in their name are all too often those who refuse that basic right to their citizens. Similarly, 'the people' is a term hijacked by those who would have us believe that they rule in our name rather than for their own self-interest and that of their cronies. In truth, where a country is truly democratic or a leader really in tune with the feelings of the people, neither word is necessary because nobody needs to be bamboozled into thinking that their impression, culled from the facts alone, could be wrong. 'Ethical' is another such word. Apart from a fund manager who needs to inform potential investors of the guiding moral precepts incorporated in the management of invested money, nobody needs to declare themselves ethical. They do, however, need to communicate clearly so that suppliers, shareholders, workers or customers can make judgements based on valid information. Equally, they must act honestly at all times even when the truth is not entirely suited to the needs of the moment. And, perhaps underpinning all that, they must act decently in all their dealings with and treatment of others.

Most obviously, ethics relates to the effect of some products and services on the behaviour and lifestyle of people. For instance, the manufacture and distribution of alcohol and tobacco or the provision of facilities for gambling are all areas where investors who take an ethical stance would not wish to place their money. It is not simply the provision of addictive opportunities to users who might have other more pressing calls on their resources such as family housekeeping. It is also the promotion of those products and services as if they were glamorous lifestyle additions when, at best, they simply cost money for a quick rush and, at worst, they can become addictive in a pernicious way and can have a corrosive effect on individuals' and families' lives. Investors with an ethical agenda would wish to avoid businesses trading in those products and services (*see* Chapter 4).

Cute little things

But it is not only people whose quality of life can be affected by the actions of companies and other organizations. At least, one might think, people can stand up for themselves. Now, while that is not always true, it is certainly not the case that animals can stand up for themselves. Some of the better publicized and more vocally contested ethical issues centre on the treatment of animals whether it be the conditions in which they are housed or the manner in which they are exploited and even killed. It is not necessary to be a vegetarian in order to find some methods of animal husbandry and slaughter unacceptably cruel. From battery farming to slaughter without stunning or bleeding an animal to death, ethical investors would tend not to wish any of their money to be used in supporting those activities. Where companies become involved in areas such as the transportation and conditions of life for veal calves or for battery chickens, the concern is often that they do not properly check on the conditions in which animals are transported or sold. Equally, most investors who wish to include ethical considerations in their investment criteria would be against the use of animals for entertainment, whether that is having to behave unnaturally in circuses or being pursued and killed for 'sport'. They would not wish to invest in any business which contributed to such activities. However, the treatment of animals does also give rise to one of the dilemmas facing ethical investment fund managers (*see* Chapter 7) and that is in the area of animals used in research. While no ethical investor would wish to derive their return from a business that used animals in testing cosmetics, when it comes to using animals in

> *It is certainly not the case that animals can stand up for themselves.*

legitimate medical research, opinions are divided between those who see animal-based research as a necessary evil and would invest to ensure that they had the power to monitor the treatment of the animals and those who are against even that.

Playing God

An area where there are growing ethical concerns is around the science of genetic engineering. Whether they believe in God or the balance of nature, many ethically concerned investors would not wish to involve their money in any business based on or associated with changing the natural order of things. On a purely practical front, many would argue that we tamper with any element of the fabric of life at our peril because we can never know the full interconnecting picture of cause and effect. Tampering with the genes of a tomato here might start a chain which ends with an incurable condition there. There is an old saying that a butterfly moves its wing and starts a chain of events culminating in a hurricane. We may never know and that, for many people, is reason enough not to interfere.

An area where there are growing ethical concerns is around the science of genetic engineering.

Good behaviour

A particular area of ethics and one which has a great deal of influence on socially responsible investors is that of corporate governance. This area of concern has always existed but came to the fore in the public's perception with the growth in influence of free market policies, as espoused by Margaret Thatcher and Ronald Reagan in the 1980s and soon taken up by most governments around the world. The policy of removing government direction from industry and of privatizing any undertakings of the state which did not directly contribute to the government of the country (and one or two that did) created massive private sectors and, in the case of former state industries, some enormous companies and lucrative monopolies. The removal of controls on capital movements created a free global market in capital compelling management teams to adopt policies to attract and maintain investment which could now move to almost any part of the world. One result was to rekindle a buccaneering spirit in many boardrooms and that, in turn, led to some lowering of corporate standards where very large amounts of money were concerned. Falsely inflating a share price through getting one's friends to buy and then using the inflated price to underpin a take-over bid for a competitor, such as was the basis of concern in the Guinness take-over of Distillers; abusing privileged information (gained from a shared system) about a competitor's activities in order to undermine that company's efforts, such as happened in the case of British Airways misusing ticketing information shared with Virgin Atlantic; these are not the activities of moral businesses and investors with ethical concerns would avoid any company while it indulged in such practices.

Stakeholders

Of course, any abuses of power and position were carried out to maximize the share price and thus benefit shareholders. However, while nobody would deny that shareholders must be able to make a fair return on their money in order to ensure that they continue to make it available, they are not the only contributors identified in the broader view of what makes a company tick and succeed. A successful business is now seen as the successful outcome of a recipe using various ingredients supplied by many people – nowadays called stakeholders. Corporate governance looks at behaviour in respect of each of those ingredients and stakeholders.

Businesses have to buy in materials and components from which to fashion their end products or with which to deliver their services. Although it may seem good for profits today to secure the lowest possible price for materials and components or to pay only long after any credit period has expired, an investor or fund manager with an ethical approach might take a different view. Notwithstanding the moral argument against so capriciously undermining somebody's livelihood, if the policy keeps putting suppliers out of business, then lack of continuity will almost certainly lead to lack of quality which will eventually have a negative effect on sales, customer satisfaction and profitability. Investors may also consider it morally wrong to exploit a weak position in poorer parts of the world in order to source materials and components at the lowest possible price. If those are your concerns, then you may wish to invest your money with a fund manager who supports companies that practise fair trade policies, avoids screwing the lowest price out of third world suppliers and either avoids child labour or ensures that education programmes are put in place to add value to the lives of working children. You may also wish to be assured that any company in which your money is invested pays its suppliers in full and on time.

You may wish to invest your money with a fund manager who supports companies that practise fair trade policies.

The conditions for the workforce in a business are key factors for ethically focused investors. Are people paid properly and do they have decent holidays? Are health and safety requirements taken seriously and fully implemented? Is worker input of ideas encouraged and rewarded? Do the workforce have a means to share in any additional value created through their efforts and are all workers, from the chief executive down, treated as equals? Are sales and marketing policies based on honesty and is after-sales service treated with as much concern as sales? Are the products safe both as to the materials used and the assembly of the finished product?

But not this

There are, though, some matters which, while they may give rise to high levels of passion, indignation and controversy, are not matters which should concern the true socially responsible investor. Most notable is politics. If a business has been privatized out of state ownership and is now competing in the market for investment funds, it should be judged purely on its merits as a business today and not in the light of any personal or political objection to the process of privatizing state-owned assets. Equally, if a business includes media interests which are felt to lean to one side or the other in politics, unless that leaning is towards anti-democratic, racist or other intolerant positions, then it should make no difference to the judgement of a socially responsible investor. In a similar vein, neither religion nor fashion are true guides as to the acceptability or otherwise of a business.

Crossover

Hopefully, this chapter has helped to set out the socially responsible investment landscape, the social investment ethos and some of its principle landmarks. The topic could warrant a book of its own and the reader is recommended to undertake further reading through organizations who specialize in finding and setting out information in this area which, like any other area of business, is always changing. Inevitably, no investor looks at any of the credentials or concerns in isolation and so there is a great deal of crossing over between the main concerns. For instance, it would be rare for environmental concerns not to give rise to ethical and corporate governance issues as the attitude which would condone pollution would be unlikely to operate strict management systems to ensure best practices in other parts of the enterprise. Therefore, while it is useful to segregate credentials and concerns in order to understand them better, it is also important, once that understanding has been achieved, to think about how they interact. Most importantly, such credentials and concerns do not run against the grain of normal life or common sense. To be concerned that your profit does not derive from the exploitation of somebody else or from the despoiling of the earth is not to say that you do not want profit. However, one great service that a strong socially concerned investment movement can render is to deny management teams the lazy options to generate revenue and profit and to ensure that any action is considered in full, even (to the extent that they can be foreseen) those ramifications that may arise in years ahead. Socially concerned investors do not wish to lose their money; they simply wish to use their money to derive a fair and honest profit through adding value as part of the process of the business rather than through taking value from other people, businesses or places.

Chapter 4

THE DIFFERENT PRIORITIES OF FUND MANAGERS

Just another investment criterion

The array of concerns to which socially responsible fund managers refer when constructing and managing ethical and environmental funds can initially appear bewildering and might even make the whole matter of investing with a conscience appear rather complex but, on the contrary, nothing could be further from the truth. It is the variety of concerns that define the investment areas where investors wish to make an impact, the clarity that an understanding of specific concerns can add to fund management as well as the levels of research and knowledge required to ensure a full understanding of investors' concerns and the ability to match the priorities of potential investments that underpin the greatest strengths of socially responsible investment. All investment funds operate within parameters which are spelled out and from which investors can easily understand the fund's priorities. For instance, a property fund would always hold most of its value in property, a Far East fund in the Far East and a natural resources fund in natural resources. However, within those broad groups there will be closer definitions relating to methods of stock selection, financial security of a potential investment business, capitalization, creditworthiness and future expectations; the quality of management and likely market for the business's product or service and a number of other requirements confirming to investors that fund managers are caring for the investment with the same concern as those whose money it is would exercise if they had the know-how or time. Equally, the presence of a prospectus will enable investors to judge whether a fund operates a policy in line with their own objectives and ensure that the managers remain in the investment area that the investors wanted, with the exception of some cash liquidity and possibly some fixed interest stocks for balance, flexibility and security. The managers of socially responsible funds are no different except that they add to these largely financial and market-focused investment concerns a further dimension of moral position. Inevitably, the priorities of socially responsible fund managers will look very similar to the priorities of socially responsible investors except that, as with any investment fund, they will be privy to the latest and most complete information and based on what is achievable as well as what will prosper as an investment.

I believe, we believe

We have already confirmed that there are as many moral or principled views about most human activities as there are people holding those views – more if anybody is indecisive or of a changeable disposition. But when it comes to investments, we could not each find a fund that exactly matched our own priorities unless we created one just for ourselves. Nevertheless, most socially responsible investors will be able to find funds that closely match their broad views and even that are in accord with their more specific concerns. If we look at the subjects and stands by which funds are defined, there are some clear similarities and relationships. Our concerns can be categorized, which does make life easier for investment managers when deciding the priorities of a fund as there are a number of clearly defined issues of concern. In the first place, there are personal concerns over which individuals may hold diametrically opposed views and which emanate from those subjects supposedly barred from polite dinner party conversation: religious beliefs, political views and ethical standards. These subjects usually give rise to passionately held positions which owe as much to a visceral sense of what is felt to be right and wrong as to any logic, although that suggestion in itself has been known to fuel similar passions. Because of their very personal nature, these individual concerns are probably the most influential drivers of socially responsible investment.

The concept itself sprang from the concerns of people, for whom their religion was at the centre of their lives. Indeed, many of the principles of profit without greed or harm to others were apparent in the way the great Victorian Quaker and Methodist commercial dynasties ran their businesses. Nowadays we sometimes hear their methods decried as paternalism but, at the time, they offered, to those families who worked for them, an infinitely improved lifestyle compared to the normal conditions of the day. Many of today's proponents of investment with a conscience will be guided by ideals which are often expressed as political beliefs and this can be a problem when selecting an investment. Also, as a reaction to the perceived greed and marginal honesty of the 1980s, many people harbour concerns about the ethics of traditional approaches to profitability in business.

> *Many people harbour concerns about the ethics of traditional approaches to profitability in business.*

After individual concerns, there are some generally applicable principles which may be discerned in socially responsible investment – matters such as health and safety, honesty and the necessity to get in tune with certain future realities in areas such as legislation or the requirement for profitability from sustainable activities. Of course, there will always be those who disagree with a particular view but, in these generally applicable areas, most people would at least pay lip service to the principles even if they continue to ignore them in order to maximize profit today with no regard for the future.

The specific nature of concerns overlays both individual and generally accepted principles. Some will be concerned with ethical issues, some with environmental issues and some with broader social concerns. All of these are dealt with elsewhere in this book and all come together to provide ethical investment with a matrix of concerns and influences which make it not only an investment of conscience but also an investment sector in which individuals will find it very easy to judge funds against the benchmark of their own beliefs and principles. It is no more than a good investment principle to know the nature of your investment and to select a fund manager who will manage the fund and wield its financial clout in a way with which you would be comfortable, in a way in which you would run it yourself if you had the skills to do so.

So, what are the main concerns that socially responsible fund managers avoid and what are the principles they support? How do they deploy the influence and strong voice of collective money? Not all funds will avoid or support companies involved in all concerns but, through the balances they achieve, they broaden the opportunities for investors with a conscience to find the right place for their money where its influence will be an extension of their own influence. Of course, the list, for all its length, is not exhaustive and the idea of breaking concerns down into categories does not mean that there is not a great deal of overlap between them. Nevertheless, the following should help readers who have yet to crystallize their own ideas to identify issues which they feel are more important.

Alcohol

This is one of those concerns whose roots may be traced back to the religious influences which initially shaped much of the socially responsible investment scene. It is not a matter of being killjoys about a substance which most of us enjoy to a greater or lesser degree but it does refer to the very real direct and indirect harm that alcohol can inflict on us all and these days it particularly refers to the pernicious social fallout from excess drinking. The effects of alcoholism are among the largest charges on the state, requiring the diversion of massive amounts of our tax revenues and the public service resources to wasteful and unproductive activities. From the cost of sending an ambulance crew to assist a fallen drunk or of sending police officers to a drunken brawl to the consequences of delay when an overstretched service fails to respond in good time to a genuine emergency, society pays a high price for alcohol misuse. It ranges from the economic loss incurred when a worker is unable to perform due to drink, to the risk of injury when such a person uses dangerous equipment or to the human tragedy of a family deprived of food, security and the routine comforts of life because somebody is spending the money on drink. It would be difficult to argue against the notion that finite resources might be better employed

The effects of alcoholism are among the largest charges on the state.

in positive support and development of society than in picking up the pieces from what is, in some people, an addiction every bit as damaging as drugs. Think of the lethal cocktail that results when drink is mixed with the motor car.

However, as the prohibition experience of 1920s America and the current experience with drugs illustrate, simply to ban a substance or to cut off legitimate supply lines is to lend it spurious cachet and allure, to make its production and distribution an underground and immensely profitable criminal activity. A reasonable approach which recognizes the rights of those who do not abuse alcohol while endeavouring to protect those weaker spirits from its influence is more likely to work. Those whose ethical concerns would prevent them from lending support to companies involved in the manufacture, import or distribution of alcoholic drinks will find most socially responsible funds share their views and avoid companies in the drinks trade although to different degrees from absolute embargoes to a limit on the degree of involvement they will find acceptable. Alcohol-related businesses are, after all, enormous operations ranging from producers of drink to the owners of hotels and family restaurant chains. Also, the tax that alcohol sales generate for governments would be difficult to replace at short notice.

In the past, individual investors have expressed less concern about alcohol than have churches and related organizations; however, there seems to be a growing awareness of the role of drink in many of society's ills and the introduction of 'Alcopops', targeted at under-age drinkers, has crystallized the previously latent concerns of ordinary folk.

Tobacco

From a situation in the infamous 1960s to the position today, one of the most significant shifts in first world public opinion has been that in the attitude to tobacco. Once regarded as a sign of social sophistication, tobacco consumption is nowadays more likely to be associated with its proven role in the development of heart and lung infections, many cancers and especially lung cancer where smoking is responsible for 90 per cent of deaths. Some estimates are that tobacco accounts for 100,000 deaths each year in the UK alone. There is also evidence that the group most likely to take up smoking is young teenage girls who, according to research published in 1998, will be most vulnerable to small cell lung cancer, the disease's most virulent form which kills within months and is almost always found in smokers.

The economic argument against tobacco is quite a difficult one as, like alcohol, it accounts for a significant part of tax revenue in some countries and is a significant industry in employment terms. According to figures from EIRIS, the value of the tobacco market in the UK alone increased from 1993 (£11.4 billion) to 1996 (£12.3 billion). That makes tobacco a very significant part of the economy and so it may only be through the exercise of financial pressure that the companies involved will ever seek to change their ways. However, there is some evidence that tobacco companies do not see their stock in trade as being

Tobacco accounts for 100,000 deaths each year in the UK alone.

permanent. Most have diversified into other areas, such as British American Tobacco's (BAT) massive involvement in the financial services market (now merged with Zurich Life but shareholders retain the value) and that may reflect the long-term trend away from smoking in western societies. Also, mergers, such as the one between BAT and Rothmans, may suggest that the companies wish their tobacco activities to form a smaller proportion of their overall business. In the short term though, companies are looking for new markets in the third world in order to continue their core source of manufacturing and distribution revenue for as long as possible and the morality of this will keep socially responsible fund managers away from the industry for the foreseeable future.

Another influence may also be the spate of legal and voluntary constraints on smoking in both public places and places of work, as well as the legal cases being brought against companies for damages resulting from consumption of tobacco by people who claim not to have been made aware of the potential dangers to their health. Neither situation is clear-cut. Constraints on any legal activity are seen by many, including a lot of non-smokers, as unjustified affronts to the civil liberties of those involved. On the other hand, there is a strong body of evidence and medical opinion pointing to the damage that passive smoking (breathing the expelled air of smokers) can cause to the health of those who do not themselves partake of the activity and that supports the notion that the civil liberties of non-smokers are just as important as those of smokers. As far as the claims of smokers for the damage rendered to their health are concerned, some may wonder where these people were for the past thirty or so years, but a less circumspect attitude might be taken towards those who claim that passive smoking in the course of their work has harmed their health. In the USA, government and the tobacco industry had reached an agreement on compensation for victims of tobacco-related diseases but that was scuppered when the government side to the deal tried to change the terms after an agreement had been reached. In the UK, lawyers acting for cancer-afflicted smokers suing tobacco companies withdrew the actions in early 1999 when faced with the prospect of picking up the tobacco producers' legal bills.

While there is a ban on tobacco advertising in many countries, the use of tobacco money to sponsor sporting activities is still allowed although there are plans to wind that down over the next ten years in the European Union. The mess into which the UK government was plunged when it exempted tobacco sponsorship of motorsport from a general rule on the matter shows how powerfully influential the tobacco companies remain and how, by locking themselves into a whole range of commercial and sporting activities, they have built that influence against the tide of public opinion. That diversification of tobacco companies into other areas of activity is one of the difficulties faced by socially responsible fund managers when considering any investments as even seemingly safe businesses may have shareholders with tobacco industry connections.

Gambling

Although no substance is involved, gambling can wreak every bit as much havoc on families and individuals as can alcohol or tobacco. As with those concerns, gambling is not a cut and dried matter. There is a fine line between restraining people from activities which may harm them and restricting their right to conduct themselves in a manner of their own choosing as long as the activity is within the law, causes no harmful effects to others and incurs no cost to the state. There is also a fine line between the rights of the individual to pursue whatever lifestyle they please and the rights of their family and society to expect them to fulfil their obligations and meet their responsibilities before any self-gratification. But the issues go deeper than that.

Gambling can wreak every bit as much havoc on families and individuals as can alcohol or tobacco.

Many fear that those who gamble the highest proportion of their income are also those who can least afford the cost and consequence loss. And, again as with alcohol and tobacco, there is a real concern that some types of gambling in amusement arcades deliberately appeal to teenagers or younger children with the aim of 'hooking' them onto a gambling habit at a young age. The problem is not only the moral issue of gambling itself but the fact that many workless young people turn to crime to finance their addiction. It often seems that those who gamble also drink and smoke to an unreasonable degree and the need to find funds for all three must be a significant motivation behind much petty crime. Meanwhile, gambling enterprises have often been associated with groups who are also connected with organized crime.

Alcohol, tobacco and gambling can offer harmless pleasure to those who use them wisely. However, they can equally have the most devastating social effects in the wrong hands.

But it is not only gambling itself that gives rise to concern these days. Football pools have been around for a long time offering the possibility, however remote, of acquiring the kind of fortune which, in former times, would have had to be inherited through a wealthy family. The cost is basically small although some people do increase their outlay by purchasing many permutations on the basic theme of trying to predict which football matches will result in scored draws. Along with the concern for families of gamblers deprived of the resources they need, there is a real concern that the idea of easy money can devalue the work ethic and that money which has been won rather than earned may do more harm than good. However, others would take the view that winning is no different from becoming a pop star and that where money does harm, it is simply bringing out the worst in already flawed people.

The advent of the National Lottery has seen gambling employed to fund a variety of causes which have previously relied on direct public donations. This has meant an increase in funding for some causes which might not otherwise have caught the public sympathy. At the same time, others whose fund-raising efforts have always been productive, have found themselves unable to raise as much as before from a public who seem to believe that participating in the lottery is the same as giving to charity. Furthermore, the lower age limit of 16 for the National Lottery (most gambling has an age limit of 18 and over) has, in the opinion of many people, encouraged young and under-age gamblers. Nevertheless it has to be said that, before the lottery, many charities did employ similar weekly draws and scratchcard programmes (albeit for much lower value prizes) to raise funds so that there may be a political rather than a moral element in some of the concerns that have been expressed.

Nevertheless, gambling carries a lot of worrying baggage for those who feel it is immoral to profit from the weakness of others even when they have freely entered into the programme. Investors who would like the use of their money to reflect their concerns about gambling will find that most socially responsible funds would agree.

Pornography and adult entertainment

There is one other exploited human weakness which investors with conscience would prefer to avoid and that is the pornography and adult entertainment business. Apart from its tendency to corrupt readers and viewers by pandering to their basest *Pornography often* drives, pornography often involves the *involves the exploitation* exploitation of people who need money *of people who need* and can only see a way to meet that need *money.* by trading their bodies. Even worse, it often exploits vulnerable people such as children who can all too easily be forced against their will into situations and actions that may demean, harm or even kill them.

Apart from the immediate and obvious issues, pornographic material may well incite weak-minded individuals to commit horrific acts of depravity and cruelty while mimicking what they have read or viewed. There is evidence that, for instance, child abusers use pornographic material to suggest to their victims that the abuse is, in fact, quite normal behaviour. For obvious reasons, those concerned to counteract the exploitation of women are opposed to pornography as women are by far the most exploited group.

Hard though it may seem, though, there are even two sides to this concern. Many of the women and increasing numbers of men who perform in strip-tease acts at pubs, clubs and other places of entertainment would claim to be happy in their work while some students of society would say that, just as bullfighting is claimed to act as a release valve for unhealthy tendencies towards violence, so strip-tease satisfies some baser instincts that might otherwise be exercized in less healthy ways. Also, in some countries, prostitution is tolerated or legal on the grounds that, with their trade regulated and in the open, those involved will have an incentive to conduct their business properly and that access to prostitutes will save men from wandering into relationships that could ultimately harm their families.

Of course, very few businesses built on pornography would find their way onto the market (with the exception of magazines) but fund managers will also be careful to avoid those Internet service providers and telephone service providers who do not take sufficient steps to ensure that material transmitted over their systems is not offensive, dangerous or available to children whom it might corrupt.

Human rights

Although pornography is one form of human rights abuse, it is part of a larger problem. Many investors first articulated their concerns not to invest their money in places where it might be used to further practices of which they disapproved when they thought about the human rights abuses associated with the apartheid regime in South Africa. For many years, socially aware fund managers avoided South Africa in order to maximize the economic consequences for the ruling minority in that country of continuing along a path which reduced the majority of the population to the status of a sub-species, little more than a productive unit for the economy. So countries with a poor record on human rights would not normally be regarded as suitable investment areas for socially responsible fund managers, neither would multinational businesses who are seen to be exploiting the people in those countries or avoiding their more general obligations towards

Countries with a poor record on human rights would not normally be regarded as suitable investment areas for socially responsible fund managers.

workers by operating with regimes who will ignore poor and dangerous work conditions as long as the ruling group is able to prosper.

One recent example that has earned the company in question a great deal of harmful publicity and has brought about a change in its practice has been the operations of Shell Oil in Nigeria. Nigeria's record on human rights was so bad that even in the Commonwealth, a majority of nations found it unacceptable enough to warrant suspending the regime's membership of that group. Shell's operations in the country were felt to be using the low value put on human life by the regime to get away with practices that would have been outlawed in other countries. There were also concerns about the company's environmental performance with news bulletin images of unattended and unsafe dumps of toxic chemicals (whether or not they were Shell's) giving a very bad impression. At the company's AGM in 1997, a shareholder resolution calling for the board and management to address the problems received 11 per cent of the vote while a further 6 per cent abstained from supporting the board. Shell is by no means alone in the criticism it has received for the manner in which it conducts business in the third world and Nigeria is not alone among countries whose regimes are felt to be abusing human rights. It is only fair to report that the elections in 1999 brought the hope of democracy for Nigeria. Indeed, it is not only in the third world that such issues of human rights abuse.

While avoiding such regimes is the usual response of investors with conscience, some are seeking to invest in enterprises which buck the trend in those countries so that the influence of money can make doing the right thing a better option than doing the wrong thing.

Inevitably, a large dose of politics comes into this area with some investors being outraged about the human rights abuses of those they oppose while seeming to be unaware of the similar faults in the regimes of those they support. A case which illustrated this would be the 1998 arrest of the former Chilean dictator, General Pinochet, to face charges arising from the undoubted human rights abuses perpetrated under his economically successful regime while the equally awful and, in terms of the economy, wholly negative actions of the government he deposed are largely ignored. The current Chilean regime, while not condoning the abuses, has decided to draw a line under the matter in order that the country can move forward and many in the third world view the actions of the British government as a paternal, almost imperialist, interference in the affairs of another nation. Socially responsible investment must not be a vehicle for moral imperialism; it should always take account of the reality on the ground in a situation where, while past wrongdoers may walk free, the country now needs all the help it can get to build a strong, democratic economy.

Socially responsible investors may well wish to select a fund in which their money can say what they believe.

Although many countries would profess to have human rights as a key influence in their dealings with other countries at any level, the reality is that money talks and so socially responsible investors may well wish to select a fund in which their money can say what they believe.

Health and safety at work

In one way, a failure to provide healthy and safe working conditions is a form of human rights abuse but it is a very specific issue. Most modern first world societies have enacted legislation governing the minimum conditions that an employer should provide to ensure that workers can do their jobs safely and without detriment to their health. These may relate to emissions created during processes, to the proper guarding of machinery or to the requirement for training to ensure that workers understand how the machinery operates. These days, the term is being applied more broadly to include the provision of comfortable conditions and adequate light in a workplace and the need to schedule work, all so as to minimize the risk of fatigue with its immediate effect on concentration levels and consequent detrimental effect on health. Issues of health and safety are not confined to factories but would include some of the most modern office environments such as call centres, dubbed by some 'the mills of the nineties'. Health and safety is one of those growing areas of legislation where governments are taking an increasingly ethical stand. Also, there is evidence that safer workplaces are more productive workplaces where workers are motivated to produce quality output in a work environment that is designed and managed for safe, efficient operation, competing on quality at a fair price rather than price alone.

Responsible employers undertake health and safety audits to ensure that their operations are not causing or risking harm to the workforce. Certainly this is an area where companies can lose a great deal of money as trades unions are very active in taking up the cases for workers whose health or safety has been compromized by their employer's poor practice, whether through malice or simply oversight. The end result of a breach of health and safety regulations is the same whether or not it was intended. In 1992, trades unions won £229m in compensation for members affected by health and safety issues. By 1996, that figure had risen to £330m. With that level of cost, poor health and safety standards are financially foolish as well as immoral.

Unfortunately, some employers in the developed world have decided that, rather than improve their practices at home, they will move production to an area with less stringent (or less firmly implemented) health and safety regulations. So, as well as avoiding those companies whose health and safety record is poor and who therefore put the lives of workers at risk in order to build short-term profitability by lowing standards rather than by building value, managers of socially responsible funds would also be concerned about companies who moved production overseas to an area where health and safety concerns were not an issue. Health and safety is certainly an area in which the enquiries of socially responsible potential investors and current investors can motivate a business to look to practices which may often be improved at little extra expense and with the result that everybody feels better about the business.

Third World exploitation

This area of concern really runs on from health and safety but includes a great deal more. Many of the earth's resources are to be found in third world countries and yet they remain the poorest nations on earth. There are a number of reasons for this including, it has to be said, the weakness of their political systems and a tendency for corruption to cause a polarization rather than a general improvement of society when money seems too often to fill the accounts of just a few in the ruling elite. However, the developed world cannot escape blame because much of the corruption, even if it is not encouraged by multinational corporations, is an inevitable consequence of the way they deal with those countries. Some companies just do not care what happens to the money they spend in the third world as long as it is less than they would spend in the developed world.

Many of the earth's resources are to be found in third world countries and yet they remain the poorest nations on earth.

Through the operation of buying cartels, prices for third world resources are kept as low as possible, while the prices of goods sold to those countries are often far higher than need be. The products sold are often not the latest but the older lines which have fully covered their initial costs and can be highly profitable. Even more shamefully, some companies will continue selling to the third world products that have been banned in developed nations because of their poor quality, safety or health failings. The active marketing of tobacco products would be a good example of companies using those less sophisticated markets to continue deriving profits from products whose star is waning in traditional markets. Another area of concern is the sale of breast milk substitutes at high prices to people who cannot afford them and do not need them, in places where the natural immunity derived from a mother's milk will protect a child but where the water used to mix the substitute product is often impure and itself a hazard to health.

Third world debt has become something of a *cause célèbre* in recent times with the dawning realization that not only can the countries involved not afford to repay the debts but also, the very fact of the debts and the onerous repayment schedules that accompany them are preventing those nations from moving forward. The counter argument is that the countries should not have borrowed so much and should have made better use of the money to build their core industries and economy rather than fritter it on grand projects which later turned out to be white elephants. Equally, less of the money ought to have gone to the cronies of the party in power at any given time. But most of the countries in question were ill prepared for their independence and were exploited by banks who saw a chance to make some big money. We may rest assured that the banks did not enter the market out of any sense of charity. Also, many projects saw the money going straight back to developed world construction companies and manufacturers. Whatever the background, the situation today is that third world debtors cannot move forward and therefore, in the global open market, neither can the rest of the world, until something is done about the debt problem. The downturn of 1998, which started with a currency crisis in Thailand and ended with the group of seven nations having to co-ordinate rescue packages through the World Bank in order to stave off a global recession, should have been warning enough of the real cost that will ensue if third world debts are not addressed. Socially responsible fund managers would be wary of any banks who were refusing to look at debt restructuring.

But, looking on the bright side, there are companies from the developed world who operate a fair trade policy in their dealing with third world countries. They aim to pay fair prices for the quality of goods provided and may even promote good employment practices where their goods are sourced. Of course, this overlaps with one of the dilemmas of socially responsible investment. If the work is withdrawn from a third world country because work practices are poor, what good does that do for the workers who lose their jobs? It is partly to address this dilemma that fair trade businesses will endeavour to improve conditions rather than employ the sanction of withdrawing work.

Animal testing

This is an area where those dilemmas raise their heads again. Animal testing is carried out for a variety of purposes, some of which are almost universally opposed while others are quite honourably supported by a proportion of the population. While it is no part of this book's purpose to become embroiled in the finer points of 'good' and 'bad' animal testing, there is a widely accepted view that animals, as living beings, deserve to be treated with consideration and humanity but that, just as humans have, in the past, used animals for food and fur as well as to assist in work, so the use of animals to help advance the human condition is a legitimate cause. If this view prevails, then the use of animal testing to try out the properties of new cosmetic formulae or toiletries is easily seen as obscene as is their use for industrial testing while their use to test drugs is less obviously bad, assuming the drugs in question are new or offer advances on current capabilities.

Animals, as living beings, deserve to be treated with consideration and humanity.

Also, by those standards, the use of animals to help identify the cause and, through that, the cure for life-shortening conditions in humankind is regrettable but necessary, as is the use of animals to 'grow' human organs for transplant purposes. Perhaps reflecting that view, in 1998 the UK government reached an accommodation with animal testers in the UK that no more licences would be granted to test cosmetics on animals and, already, in Europe and the USA, cosmetic companies have found alternative testing methods, including a final test using human volunteers. The growing popularity of ethical products in this market (and not only among teenagers) is testimony to a growing public awareness and opinion.

Another view in this area would ban all animal testing on the grounds that humans have no right to subject animals to physically harmful or destructive processes under any circumstances. However, some of the methods used by extremists in the animal protection movement are themselves not acceptable and may be more likely to inflame public opinion against their cause than to evince any support. On the other hand, an ethical approach by managers of socially responsible funds (on behalf of their investors) should have more impact as it is difficult to whip up a story against people simply voting with their money. Reflecting the general dilemma of this issue, there are funds which do support the use of animal testing for medical research while categorizing themselves as ethical.

Intensive farming methods and the consumption of meat

There is no doubt that vegetarianism is a growing movement and no longer the preserve of cranks. Support from the likes of the late Linda McCartney made many more people aware of the possibilities of eating a healthy but meat-free diet. Issues such as the BSE crisis, which had a particularly damaging effect on the UK's economy, and its impact on the human population through the new derivative of Creutzfeld Jacob's Disease (CJD) helped to make increasing numbers of people wary of eating meat or meat derivatives. However, true vegetarians only account for about 4.5 per cent of the UK population while a further 6.7 per cent avoid red meat (figures from EIRIS). This still represents double the figures of ten years ago and there is probably a significantly larger group who will eat a meal without meat once or twice in a week.

Vegetarianism is a growing movement and no longer the preserve of cranks.

Even among people who do eat meat, there is concern over conditions in which the animals are kept and the fact that supermarkets now stock organically grown or free-range meat suggests that there is a desire for food 'with a conscience'. The problem is that food raised decently will usually cost more than factory and intensively farmed products. So socially responsible fund managers might well concern themselves not only with the production of meat through decent methods (some, of course, will avoid any meat trade) but also with companies researching ways to farm organically at less cost as well as the pricing policies of retailers who may not be paying organic farmers much more for their produce but who charge the public a great deal more.

Genetic engineering

Only recently, this might have been included with farming methods but it has lately become an issue in its own right. Scientists have discovered that, by introducing genes from other life forms into crops and animals, they can stimulate properties that seem, at first sight, to be useful. Cereal, vegetable and fruit crops can be naturally proofed against insect attack by introducing the gene from another insect to the strain; cattle may grow a great deal larger if the gene from a faster growing animal is introduced into the breed. But, and it is a big but, very little if anything is known about the long-term effects on people consuming food products which have been genetically altered.

Very little if anything is known about the long-term effects on people consuming food products which have been genetically altered.

Already, in an act of unwitting genetic engineering, chemicals used to make insects infertile have been consumed by fish which have then become the food for people. Some scientists would cite this as one explanation for lower levels of fertility in human males in recent times. As with so many things, the problem with genetic engineering is that its full impact may not be known until a generation have been blighted; by then, it will be too late.

Genetic engineering is also opposed on moral grounds: that it is no part of humanity's work to interfere with the basic building blocks of life (God's work, if that is your belief), the dismantling and re-ordering of which will eat away the very basis of our existence. Socially responsible investors will wish to ensure that their money is invested where it will support improved food production by other methods than genetic engineering and will wish to avoid investment in those businesses whose activities include that branch of science.

Armaments

The ethical investment movement included, in the first instance, many people who were opposed to the use of force by the West to impose its will on the world in campaigns such as the 1956 Anglo-French venture to capture the Suez Canal and the USA's venture in Vietnam. This extended to the Russian invasion of Afghanistan and the general use of force or arming of less

It is wrong to kill and particularly wrong for a state to kill.

developed countries to carry on proxy wars for their developed world arms suppliers, as was the case in Angola and Mozambique. The more basic moral stand is that it is wrong to kill and particularly wrong for a state to kill.

Nowadays, the concerns are as much directed at the suppliers of arms to poor developing nations whose need is more for food and the means to employ their people gainfully than for the weapons to continue feuds with their neighbours, or worse. That concern extends beyond the weapons to the means to produce weapons and recent experience with Iraq has shown the folly of providing any country with the means to create a lethal arsenal. It also includes systems such as computers which might well have military applications. In particular, protesters have targeted companies selling arms to regimes who have a record of turning their weaponry on their own population. One recent example in the UK was that of protesters who broke into a British Aerospace plant and inflicted damage on Hawk jets destined for Indonesia where the government was using military weapons against its own people in East Timor. As subsequent events demonstrated, the government was by no means in power with the support of the population. Socially responsible fund managers will be careful not to invest in companies who are selling arms, the means to produce arms or the means to conduct war.

However, as we will see later in Chapter 7 on dilemmas, there is also a view that, in this post-cold war world, if some groups such as NATO and UN forces are not properly armed, then we can expect to see more horrific genocide, such as the campaign which has probably destroyed any chance of co-existence in our lifetimes between states from the former Yugoslavia. There may be a case in the future for socially responsible investors to countenance supporting businesses making weapons of restraint which cannot easily be turned into tools of aggression and which are not available to regimes who might turn them on their own people. It is, though, difficult to segregate arms to be used for peacekeeping from those to be employed for war, as the same forces are used in both events.

Nuclear energy

Perhaps it should go without saying that an ethical or socially responsible investor would want nothing to do with nuclear armaments, their production or delivery systems, but nuclear energy is used in far more

An ethical or socially responsible investor would want nothing to do with nuclear armaments.

ways than just weapons. The problem is that there does not seem to be any absolute assurance that a nuclear power plant will not cause long-term damage to the population of the area in which it is sited and there have been many 'minor' incidents plus a couple of serious ones (Three Mile Island and Chernobyl) which have caused enormous environmental and human damage. There are also legal radioactive discharges from all nuclear plants which, even though they are legal, still worry people.

The storage and reprocessing of waste and the close proximity of nuclear energy and nuclear weapons technology all add to the concern that this industry may be building up a lethal stockpile for which there is no absolutely secure or leakproof storage and no known means of disposal.

As reserves of fossil fuels decline and as we become increasingly concerned about the effects of burning those fuels to produce energy, it may be that nuclear energy will become too important to be abandoned. If so, a lot of work will need to be done before this sector could even approach the criteria for an environmentally responsible investment fund.

Greenhouse gases and ozone depletion

If we do abandon nuclear energy, the main alternative currently would be fossil fuels which relinquish their energy at a price: either the cost of containing the pollution they produce or the damage done when that pollution is released into the atmosphere. We are using up our resources at an accelerating rate; some estimate that, in the twentieth century, we have consumed more of the earth's natural wealth than in all previous history. Because much of those resources have been burnt as fuel, pollution from the smoke they produce has been constantly assailing the atmosphere since the dawn of the industrial revolution two centuries ago. What we have recently discovered is that the gases and particles in that smoke have a long-term effect on the ability of the atmosphere to disperse heat energy and that, gradually but continually, the earth is becoming warmer. Are the two phenomena linked? There are those who point to past climatic cycles long before the human race was polluting the

We are using up our resources at an accelerating rate.

air on the current scale but the problem with hoping that it is simply a natural part of the earth's cycle is that, if the theory is wrong, we will only know (or our children will only know) when it is too late. As the planet warms, so ice melts, oceans rise and land is lost to the sea. At that point, the financial cost of managing the problem would be crippling and would reduce living standards to primitive levels everywhere. Better to start addressing the problem now and, if it is one of your concerns, to ensure that your money is not invested in part of the problem – fossil fuel burning energy producers.

At the 1997 climate conference in Kyoto, Japan, some measures were agreed although these were so heavily hedged with caveats that cynics might have thought the conference did more damage through the hot air it produced than the measures it agreed could possibly counter. And the establishment of a pollution exchange in Chicago has allowed the worst offenders to 'buy' the pollution quotients of less developed countries, which must reduce their incentive to clean up their act or their air!

A particular problem for the atmosphere is the damage inflicted on the ozone layer by some chemicals released into the air. The ozone layer should surround the earth in the upper atmosphere and filter out from the sun's rays the harmful ultraviolet radiation that is believed to cause skin cancers and cataracts, and is blamed, by some, for damage to marine food chains and crops. An accumulation of ozone-depleting chemicals, including the well known CFC gas from refrigeration units and aerosols, has destroyed some of that ozone layer until it has become dangerously thin, particularly over the North and South Poles where it has been found to 'tear' at certain times. CFCs are no longer produced in developed nations but, because the alternatives are regarded as expensive, the date for finally ceasing production world wide has not been set until the year 2015.

Investors with environmental concerns would usually not wish their money to be invested in any company that contributed to this problem either directly by burning fossil fuels or releasing chemical pollution, or indirectly by extracting fossil fuels or the raw materials from which ozone-depleting chemicals can be made. They may, though, wish to invest in a business whose processes or products were tackling pollution.

Loss of forested areas and non-replacement of tropical hardwood

The one component in the ecological system we call earth that can repair damage done to the atmosphere is the forest. Trees convert harmful carbon monoxide into oxygen, which is why the great forests are often referred to as the lungs of the earth. Unfortunately, just as pollution levels have increased our need for lungs, we have been reducing the forested area of the earth to house, feed and employ a growing population. In particular, the great hardwood tropical rain forests with

The great forests are often referred to as the lungs of the earth.

their broad-leafed trees have the best capability of breaking down pollution but take the longest to grow. Therefore, when they are cut down, the resource is lost for decades before the next generation can grow and many other species of flora and fauna may perish when robbed of the protection, shelter and food source that great trees offer. All too often, where replacement is carried out, it is with softwood trees which grow fast but cannot reduce pollution as efficiently and may even change the composition of the soil around them, making it less hospitable for other indigenous plant species.

Socially responsible investors would not wish to support

uncontrolled deforestation, though there is a case for investing in properly managed, sustainable forests where harvesting is controlled so as to minimize the harm done and where replacement planting is standard practice. This is an area where consumers can also have an impact simply by refusing to buy wood products not certified as coming from sustainable forests which are monitored and certified by the Forest Stewardship Council which the World Wide Fund for Nature helped to establish.

Water pollution and pesticides

Of course, not all pollution goes into the atmosphere. Water is often the largest element, by volume, in an industrial process. From cooling to cleaning, water seems the ideal cheap and abundantly available carrier for heat and chemical pollution (including human waste). If, though, water is returned to the nearest river or ocean while carrying those pollutants, great damage can be done to fish, animals and plant life. Worse still, disease can be carried through the human population at an alarming rate as we see when floods break down the usual disposal systems and expose the victims to polluted water supplies. More worrying, some of the chemical cocktails now being washed into the world's rivers and oceans seem immune to the normal biological degrading which eventually breaks down more natural substances. Many socially responsible fund managers will avoid any involvement with companies who pollute the water and fail to restore its condition before returning it to the river or ocean from which it came.

But not all pollution results from energy generation or industrial production. Since World War Two, people have demanded ever more, ever more varied and ever cheaper food from a finite landmass on which our increasing population must also live and work. Given all the other things we demand, these food requirements could only be met by maximizing the use of the land and minimizing any loss of crops to natural causes. That has invariably meant using chemicals in food

Since World War Two, people have demanded ever more, ever more varied and ever cheaper food from a finite landmass.

production – chemicals to add into the land those elements that the crops require to grow and chemicals to prevent insects or disease from blighting the crop. The substances used to fertilize the land often contain hormones and chemicals which can cause very serious medical conditions if ingested directly even in trace quantities and, because they are being applied to land that is already overworked, each application does more damage to the soil and, when it is finally washed away by rain, leaves a residue even more leached of life and even more in need of chemical additives.

Pesticides are poisons; that is how they work. And, because pests build up immunity, the applications have to be in ever stronger doses. Many people are now seriously concerned at the effect on the human population of eating food treated with chemicals and investors with a concern for the environment will usually not wish to invest in any business which produces or uses such chemicals. They may, on the other hand, wish to invest in businesses which grow organically or using a permaculture system.

Roads

Nobody would deny that the internal combustion engine has been one of our more powerful inventions. By converting refined fossil fuel into motion, it has enabled us to take control of the environment for better or worse. The car has given the power of mobility to millions who in earlier ages might never have strayed more than a couple of days' walk from the place of their birth (unless with an army) and who can now enjoy the privilege of travel and the freedom to go where they please. It will be a hard act to follow. Public transport certainly cannot come near to it and it will be a brave government that will do more than tinker at the edges of our ownership and use of cars.

It will be a brave government that will do more than tinker at the edges of our ownership and use of cars.

Also, trucks have proved to be the most flexible and cost-effective door-to-door transport system for freight. Requiring no special tracks except the public roads, trucks have made possible revolutions such as the proliferation of food store hypermarkets outside our towns (mainly accessed by shoppers in cars) and the movement of perishable goods from one end of the country to the other within the day. Again, the railways really cannot compete on flexibility, ability to access any sites or price. It would again be a brave government that restricted the use of trucks for freight transport.

But, and it is a big but, the internal combustion engine emits high levels of toxic exhaust and even when running on 'clean' fuel using low emission technology, it is one of the most prolific sources of atmospheric pollution. Perhaps the only way to control it is to halt the building of new roads, use technology to increase current road capacity, charge a toll to use roads in the areas most vulnerable to pollution (mainly the big cities) and divert resources to ensure that, when motorists look for an alternative, there is one and it is an attractive one, rather than an ordeal to be endured.

Protests against new road schemes have hit the headlines in recent years but the actions of investment funds have actually brought some contractors to the point of declaring that they will not be tendering for any further road building contracts. This is also an area where socially responsible investors can support businesses who are seeking ways to resolve the problem without a too great impact on living standards.

Banking

Although banking may not at first seem to cause any ethical offence, the part played by some banks in the maintenance of the economy and regime in South Africa brought them to the attention of concerned investors. From there it became apparent that banks were not only financing bad governments but were also involved in third world debt – an issue which many regard as a burden 'sold' to developing world

Third world debt – an issue which many regard as a burden 'sold' to developing world countries to fund projects they did not require.

countries to fund projects they did not require and line the pockets of the ruling clique at the long-term expense of the country which has to repay the debt. With interest payments eating up a high proportion of the country's meagre income, many people question not only the morals but also the business sense of lending in these circumstances.

Irresponsible marketing and advertising

It's all down to honesty really. While nobody would deny the need for marketing and sales, the appeal should be based on the truth about the product or service and any surveys or research cited as evidence should be genuine independent work, not something concocted in-house with the outcome determined in advance. No sales or marketing effort should rely on the baser traits of human nature in order to create an appeal. Sex, disadvantage, race, creed – none of these should be used to sell a product or service unless the

> *No sales or marketing effort should rely on the baser traits of human nature in order to create an appeal.*

product or service is directly relevant to those subjects. Socially responsible investors would not wish their capital to be supporting a business that relied on irresponsible or misleading marketing and sales messages.

Environmental initiatives

We have already seen that socially responsible fund managers would seek to avoid investment in companies whose activities are damaging to the environment. But this is an area in which many companies are making considerable efforts to improve their performance, to make good any damage resulting from their activities, to build sustainability into their processes or to make it their business to add value to the environment. Most investors who are concerned for the environment would wish to invest in such businesses and some fund managers will take such positive investment steps as part of their policy.

A growing number of businesses are instigating environmental audits and reports as well as financial ones, and many are striving to meet the international standard in this area – ISO 14001. The companies are not just small or overtly environmentally aware ones but include such global corporations as the UK's telecommunications company – BT. Motor manufacturers are endeavouring to use components that can be easily recycled at the end of the vehicle's working life, while furniture and DIY businesses try to source their products from sustainable and managed forests rather than from operations that simply take the wood without any thought to the future. And it is not just in their products and services that companies can act. Many now make the effort to minimize the amount of energy they use and wherever possible to use systems and materials with a lower environmental impact. A good example would be the installation of heat exchange units to make use of ambient conditions, solar panels or the incineration of waste in a unit which captures the exhaust gases and produces energy from the heat.

Companies developing wind- or wave-power generators, businesses specializing in protecting or restoring habitats after or during a mining or quarrying programme, companies engaged in recycling or who have made a commitment to use only ingredients with a clean history, all these are legitimate investments for the fund manager seeking to maintain a positive policy. Of course, with all of these, the intention is good but the means to implement that intention, the will to monitor progress and act to put right any problems and the honesty to report openly on these issues are all much better guides to a business's commitment to the environment.

Not all investment criteria seek to avoid those activities deemed to be bad. A growing element of the socially responsible investment market targets businesses whose activities should be encouraged and where an investment will enable the investor to be part of the solution.

Responsible products and services, recycling, energy conservation

This is, of necessity, an imprecise area and one where individual judgements may differ as to what is good and what is not. However, by and large, it refers to products that help reduce or eliminate pollution or limit the consumption of natural resources. For instance, recent experiments have tried to develop cars with flywheel motors that can store the kinetic energy built up as a car accelerates and then release that energy as motion on less demanding stretches of road where steady speed rather than acceleration might be required. In so doing, the flywheel motor allows the car's engine temporarily to idle or even switch off. There are also a number of experimental cars, light commercial vehicles and buses being tested which either replace or supplement their internal combustion engines with electric motors. There are a number of engineering problems associated with these developments and a socially responsible investor might well wish to invest in a business that was striving to overcome those problems. Other energy-related products might be involved with developments using wind or wave power and other means of generating energy from sustainable and renewable resources.

Responsible products might assist in the process of waste disposal through, perhaps, small-scale composting units to be used with the vegetable wastes of apartment dwellers. Equally, businesses involved in the safe disposal or, ideally, the substantial recycling of waste as a useful raw material would be regarded as acceptable by most ethical and environmental screening processes.

Businesses whose products or services provide a lower impact and viable alternative to travel or other polluting activities would qualify as responsible. That is why telecommunications companies can be popular with socially responsible fund managers. Staple requirements such as affordable accommodation, heat, light, power, communication, clothing, food and drink might well fall into this category, as well as educational and general reading materials. And the provision of healthcare is another clearly responsible activity as long as it is healthcare and not for cosmetic purposes.

Help industries to set benchmarks for positive achievement rather than simply things not to do.

It is more difficult for fund managers to determine what they would like to support on behalf of investors than it is to identify what to avoid. However, as more investors seek to include a measure of social responsibility into the factors which determine where their investment should go and as the market becomes increasingly mature, to support responsible activities positively must be seen as a sensible way forward. It is also a process that, by clarifying the activities which (all other business issues being equal) socially responsible investors are prepared to support will help industries to set benchmarks for positive achievement rather than simply things not to do.

Equality of treatment and opportunity and positive employment practices

On the ethical front, there can be no reasonable person who would today oppose the principle that everybody should be treated in the same way and have access to the same opportunities, based solely on aptitude, ability and experience regardless of sex, race, colour, religion or physical ability. And yet, there is still a great deal of discrimination experienced in workplaces around the world. Women tend to work in part-time jobs and in many countries that still means they have virtually no rights or benefits, not even on a pro-rata basis whereas full-time workers do. Also, it is still the case in many countries that even well qualified people from ethnic and religious minorities find their opportunities in the job market limited or that the opportunities available are only for menial work. In some countries there are positive discrimination arrangements in force to try to ensure that each group in society has at least a level of access to opportunities equivalent to that group's proportion of the population. Some people find that patronizing, demeaning and open to the charge that people are getting jobs for reasons other than ability. It would be better if it were understood as sound business practice and good for the shareholders to open employment opportunities to the best talent available, regardless of sex, race, colour, religion or physical ability. Fund managers whose investors wish to include an ethical dimension in their investment criteria will be pleased to invest in businesses whose employment policy does just that, not only because it is morally right but also because it makes sense to employ, train and promote the best and most appropriate people for the job.

Everybody should be treated in the same way and have access to the same opportunities.

Equally, an enlightened employer who treats the workforce as valuable members of a team with ideas to contribute and deserving of a fair share of the rewards of success will be well regarded. A recent example at the time of writing was a man whose workforce were prepared to work long hours for no additional pay in order to save the kitchen manufacturing and fitting business that employed them. When, eventually, the business turned around and was sold for a handsome sum, the owner used part of the sale proceeds to clear the mortgages of all of his workforce.

Training and education

Nothing so improves a person as education and training. It enables people to realise the best in themselves and to contribute fully and satisfactorily to society. It helps people to break free from constraints of birth, upbringing and poverty. Therefore, organizations who provide education and training programmes and materials will, subject to the other screening criteria, usually be acceptable for those funds which aim to support rather than avoid.

Nothing so improves a person as education and training.

Fair trade

If an investor wishes to avoid companies that exploit third world people, then it is a logical corollary that they might wish to support companies that operate a fair trade policy. Certainly from the point of view of the people in the countries concerned, fair trade is more likely to solve their problems than a trade embargo. Fair trade businesses will endeavour to source materials and products from the third world but will be prepared to pay a price which does not encourage the worst kind of human exploitation. Often, poor conditions in third world workplaces arise in response to the need to be competitive in a cut-throat price-driven market. If, however, a buyer comes into the market who is prepared to pay a fair price for the materials and products, the financial pressure will be lifted. If, furthermore, that buyer then makes it clear that the fair price is dependent upon there being demonstrably decent working conditions in the workplace, the pressure will become positive rather than negative. Many charities will operate a fair trade policy for their trading arm to help stimulate the commercial activity that will help poor countries to be able eventually to fend for themselves without the need for aid.

Supporting the community and corporate giving

This is quite a difficult area for fund managers, as what companies support may not always coincide with what individual investors regard as worthwhile causes. It has to be accepted that much of the money that companies give is part of their marketing effort and expected either to help raise the profile of the brand or associate the business with something that potential customers will value. But, for all that, recipients are glad of the support and we should not be too cynical about the motives. In the first place, there is nothing intrinsically wrong in associating a business with a willing cause and, in the second place, a surprising amount of corporate giving has no strings attached. The philan-

> *A surprising amount of corporate giving has no strings attached.*

throphic spirit of Victorian entrepreneurs, often fuelled by religious belief and a genuine desire to share some of their wealth, is not dead. Perhaps, rather than seeking purely altruistic community involvement, it would be better to look for companies that make an effort to help the community to help itself through projects such as British Telecom's 'BT in the community' awards for local developments which will add something to the community in question, or Railtrack's similar scheme for communities near the railway. These schemes operate in the UK but similar schemes will be found across the world. At the end of the day, readers will need to find what, if any, community involvement and corporate giving a fund manager would regard as supportable.

Disclosure

Disclosure is a key indicator of the good faith of a business and many companies will declare their ethical or environmental credentials in the sorts of terms used above. But, for socially responsible investment fund managers to be impressed, fine words will need to be followed by actions, monitoring, correction where necessary and a willingness to be absolutely open about what is being done and how it is to be achieved. Issues that cause concern include how businesses operate, how they compete and how much top managers and directors earn (directly and indirectly). This may seem like pure nosiness and there is a tendency

Disclosure is a key indicator of the good faith of a business.

among some investors with a political agenda to ignore the fact that a director's income will usually reflect the satisfaction that shareholders feel at the way their investment is being handled. However, there are enough cases of incompetent directors and managers milking a company to the detriment of shareholders and workers alike for openness is this respect to be a reasonable demand in the interests of good business practice. Also, the more shares are held by investors and funds whose criteria for good management include that the business should act ethically in all its dealings and treat its workforce (from the shopfloor to the boardroom) with equality, the more companies will wish to act properly and be open about that fact.

Public transport

Although politicians and others talk about penalising the use of cars to reduce traffic levels, the best way to achieve that and for the politicians

Offer travellers a system of public transport that does not seem like a downmarket alternative to using the car.

who bring it about to stay in office, is to offer travellers a system of public transport that does not seem like a downmarket alternative to using the car. The reality is that there are many aspects of public transport that travellers find unpleasant or inconvenient.

Public transport is regarded by many people as an inconvenient system which requires the user to make an initial journey from home or office to the nearest joining point and another such journey at the end. People today regard time spent walking and waiting as time wasted but that might be partly offset if the public transport system, once reached, offered comfort equal to the car plus the opportunity to do some work or reading and, perhaps, drink a cup of tea.

However, not only are the vehicles often not clean, they are also overcrowded, do not even attempt to offer seats to all travellers and may be out of date and badly maintained and so prone to be unreliable. Also, their frequency is sometimes erratic; this is usually not the public transport system's fault when the roads are shared but it is very annoying when the system is a railway. Small irritations can creep in if connections have not been properly aligned – for example, the bus leaves the station forecourt one minute before the train arrives or the driver refuses to open the door to waiting passengers because it is his or her break. Last, but by no means least, public transport is often felt to be unsafe which, while it may well be more perception than reality, still has the same effect.

If an investor is serious about the need to reduce pollution from road use, then there is a lot to be said for investing in the enterprises which build the infrastructure and vehicles for public transport systems or which operate them. That would include timetabling software, security systems and other systems that can make the system more responsive to the needs of passengers. It is also likely that, as government policy moves increasingly in favour of public transport and as bulk freight transporters rediscover, courtesy of the Channel Tunnel, the value of rail transport for long distances, for exports and for bulk transport of single cargoes, businesses associated with the system will thrive.

No clear divides

The categories of activities avoided and supported by different funds serve to help investors decide whether a fund will use their money in a manner similar to how they would use it themselves. It is a guide to the priorities of the fund but should not be taken as evidence that a fund has no view on matters beyond those priorities. The managers of socially responsible funds will all avoid nuclear energy or activities which damage the environment, and will all take a generally ethical or environmentally sensitive approach to the way they view potential investments. And, of course, there is a great deal of overlap between the categories above.

To assist in the task of deciding which companies might join their list of potential investments (remember, investment targets still have to pass muster on the normal grounds of financial performance and potential for growth and income, even if they are socially responsible), most fund managers employ a screening process, not to judge companies but to assess the extent to which their actions match their stated policy. This screening process helps fund managers to reduce the universe of potential investments to manageable proportions and can be weighted to identify potential investments which share the ethical and/or environmental priorities of the fund.

In 'Money and Ethics', EIRIS breaks down the main priorities to a number of issues and subdivisions against which to check each of the funds who claims to include that priority in the investment criteria.

Passive becomes active

In the United States of America, a new type of ethical fund is emerging, one which seeks companies which are not doing the right things but over which the fund, on behalf of its investors, wishes to wield some influence. This pro-active approach may well be the way of the future as it does not need a majority of or even many shares to have an influence. Trades union members in the UK and members of organizations such as Friends of the Earth sometimes buy one share each in order to be able to attend a company's annual general meeting (AGM) to raise the issue about which they are concerned and put before other shareholders any facts, expert opinions and arguments which support their stance on the issue. The very fact of airing the view, the media attention it attracts and the value of bringing an issue to the notice of other shareholders can start a process of change that gathers pace until it becomes irresistible. Shell Petroleum found that out when a few protesters holding an infinitesimal number of shares managed first to get the issue of oil rig disposal and, in particular, the disposal of the Brent Spar platform, aired at the AGM, into the public arena and onto the agendas of institutional shareholders so that Shell, seeing the way things were going, changed its policy and launched reforms which should see the company among the most enlightened organizations in years to come (although still an extractor of non-renewable resources).

Although the overall ethical and environmental approach is similar in all such funds, each manager of a socially responsible fund will have his or her own priorities which makes it more likely that an investor will find a fund *There are many criteria by which priorities can be set.* with priorities to which he or she can sign up. The length of this chapter shows that there are many criteria by which priorities can be set and that is further evidence of the detailed understanding that fund managers in this sector must have in order to do their job properly.

Part 2

HOW DO I BECOME A
CONCERNED INVESTOR?

Chapter 5

HOW INVESTORS CAN SORT OUT THEIR OWN CONCERNS

Organized beliefs

Of course, generalities are useful but only so far. If you would prefer your investments to be in tune with your own beliefs about what is right and what is wrong, to support that which you support and avoid that which you eschew, then you will need, at some stage, to organize those beliefs. This may sound a little callous for an investment philosophy which is about broader values than profit alone, although it must be emphasized that there is nothing wrong with profit as long as it is decently obtained and results from a true added value rather than being the other side of somebody else's loss or the sequestering of future value. Indeed, it is

There is nothing wrong with profit as long as it is decently obtained.

in the hope of profit that most people conduct their working and investing lives although not all would measure that profit in just monetary terms. Nevertheless, given the wide choice of funds available and the wide range of priorities that they have incorporated to their standards and protocols, if the investors have not analyzed and organized their own beliefs, however are they going to know which fund managers will invest in the way that will support those beliefs?

What do you think?

Sorting out personal concerns is not a difficult job. Many people will start by writing down those issues which can make them think when, for instance, they come up as an item in the news. Are you moved by events which involve and affect people or do you find your own feelings run strongest when places and artefacts are threatened? When you hear of a coal mine closing, do you inwardly rejoice that there will be one less slag heap scarring the countryside and wonder how the land will be restored? Or do you despair for the families whose livelihood has been cut away and wonder whether there will be any new development on the site to restore the dignity of work and maintain the spirit of a community? If your first concern is for the land, then the environment may be your prime motivation while those who think first of the people may have an ethical emphasis in their concerns. Neither is better than the other and each could argue the case for their own view being the one that would secure the long-term good of the community. Of course, it is perfectly possible to hold a combination of those feelings and wish for a sensible outcome that will balance the

Sort out your own priorities.

desire to restore the land with a pragmatic acceptance that there will need to be new development but in a manner that is sympathetic to the area. Are there particular issues about which, for one reason or another, you feel passionately? Have you lost a loved one in an industrial accident and now wish to ensure that employers do not play fast and loose with health and safety? Has your community been cut in half by road building and subsequently seemed to lose its cohesion and that spirit that marks out a community from a collection of buildings and people? Have you experienced at close hand the devastation that alcohol and gambling can wreak or lost a dear relative to cancer or another condition following a lifetime of cigarette smoking or working in a toxic environment? Do you find yourself moved by the plight of people in faraway places being killed and injured by munitions that have been manufactured in this country? It may take an afternoon or even more to sort out your own priorities. Like most concerned people, you may be surprised at how many matters there are over which you would like to effect some influence for change. But, with the best will in the world, you will not be able to address them all and so you ought to ascribe a score (say, out of ten) to each concern in order to impose an order and a set of priorities.

One technique is initially to use the method applied by market researchers of ascribing to each possibility a weighted view. It works

Figure 5.1
ORGANIZING YOUR BELIEFS

Concerns	Strongly agree	Agree	Neither agree nor disagree	Disagree	Strongly disagree
To oppose and avoid					
Alcohol					
Tobacco					
Gambling					
Pornography and adult entertainment					
Human rights					
Health and safety at work					
Third world exploitation					
Animal testing					
Intensive farming and consumption of meat					
Genetic engineering					
Armaments					
Nuclear energy					
Greenhouse gases and ozone depletion					
Loss and non-replacement of forests					
Water pollution and pesticides					
Roads					
To support					
Environmental initiatives					
Responsible products and services					
Equality of treatment and opportunity					
Fair trade					
Supporting the community and corporate giving					
Disclosure					

Figure 5.2
MATCHING YOUR BELIEFS TO A FUND

Concerns	Name of fund	Notes	Match Yes or No?	
			Ideal	This fund
To oppose and avoid				
Alcohol				
Tobacco				
Gambling				
Pornography and adult entertainment				
Human rights				
Health and safety at work				
Third world exploitation				
Animal testing				
Intensive farming and consumption of meat				
Genetic engineering				
Armaments				
Nuclear energy				
Greenhouse gases and ozone depletion				
Loss and non-replacement of forests				
Water pollution and pesticides				
Roads				
To support				
Environmental initiatives				
Responsible products and services				
Equality of treatment and opportunity				
Fair trade				
Supporting the community and corporate giving				
Disclosure				

like this. Take each belief covered in Chapter 4, plus any other that may be particular to your own concerns, and write it down as a statement starting either with the phrase 'I support . . .' or 'I am against . . .'. Hence, you might say, 'I support fair trade' or 'I am against animal testing for non-medical purposes.' Alongside each statement write a number as follows:

1 I strongly agree with the statement
2 I agree with the statement
3 I neither agree nor disagree with the statement
4 I disagree with the statement
5 I strongly disagree with the statement

Figure 5.1 provides an example of how the table might look.

Now group the statements according to their scores and you will be able to identify your main and secondary concerns – 'strongly agree' and 'agree' – from the issues over which you have little or no concern – the rest. You could, of course, further refine the list by applying a similar exercise to each group until all concerns are listed in a sequence but, quite honestly, life is too short.

Then, it might be a useful exercise to create the investment terms of your ideal fund in much the same way that fans create ideal combinations and teams in fantasy sport competitions. While you are unlikely to find a fund run along exactly the lines which you would follow, you will at least now have a starting point from which to work. Figure 5.2 provides an example of how the table might look.

Pick an investment

Apart from their investment strategy and objectives, funds are operated under different sets of rules depending on the purposes for which investors will use them. You may already be familiar with the different types of fund available. If, however, you are a relative novice to the world of investment, then it may be useful to understand what different funds are and how they work. This section cannot be anything more than a brief review of each investment type available in the UK. But even before that, we should take a brief look at shares, although not the wilder reaches of the market where futures, options and other exotica are generally felt to be the preserve of the expert and the wealthy expert at that. But a concerned investor can invest in shares directly. Frankly, this would not be a good option for most UK investors because minimum dealing charges are generally disproportionately high on small portfolios while, unless quite a large sum of money is involved, it would be difficult to achieve the safety of a spread of shares. Also, unless it is a hobby to keep up to date with the markets, it will be difficult to know how to evaluate and select stocks as well as knowing when to sell. Selling is the critical transaction through which paper profits and losses become real values and costs to the bank balance. Most (not all) individual investors get selling wrong and most (not all) institutional investors get it right. Nevertheless, it is possible that an investor would be as specific as wishing to support a particular business for personal reasons, in which case a purchase of shares in that business might be a good way to achieve that. However, unless you are an experienced investor who can read and understand the accounts produced by companies, this may not be a good idea. At the very least, it would be prudent to enlist and pay for the expertise of a trained accountant to provide a report on the financial and business aspects of the business. Equally, groups like trades unions and environmental campaigners sometimes buy a minimum number of shares in a business in order to be able to attend shareholder meetings and make a point. There are stockbrokers who will handle transactions for private clients and there are share shops as well as banks who will handle quite small sums for investment. Certainly in the USA and the UK as well as some Far Eastern markets, there are a lot of individual shareholders; privatization shares, where access was made deliberately easy, have brought many more investors into share markets. But ethical and environmental investment is a specialist area which means that it is usually best to take the advice of specialists with a track record. Unless there is a specific reason to support a particular business or a compelling reason to be at the AGM, shares will not be a good idea for most investors.

The next step up from shares is to use the expertise of a portfolio management service. These, again, are mainly for larger investors (most services require a minimum investment of £25,000 or more with one or two only looking at investors having £200,000 or more available). Portfolio management services can best be described as having your own unit trust and employing an investment expert to run it. Although most portfolio fund managers will invest in accordance with several pre-planned sets of criteria, some will be prepared to sit down with larger investors and discuss the exact investments which will best fit into the portfolio profile preferred by the investor. Some stockbrokers are already operating a service which includes the option to have an ethical or environmental emphasis in a portfolio. The assistant fund manager for the Ethical Development Service offered by private client stockbroker, Brewin Dolphin Bell Lawrie, explains that, 'Ethical beliefs are simply another tier in the process of establishing a client's investment priorities. We already consider whether they want income or growth and their attitude to risk and so a client's beliefs and ethical concerns [sit well with those areas].' At Brewin Dolphin Bell Lawrie, there certainly seems to be a move towards taking account of these criteria even if this entails a slight underperformance against general markets when things are going well. For all that, neither shares nor a portfolio service may be suitable for the majority of readers.

The next step up from shares is to use the expertise of a portfolio management service.

What most people fear about investing in stock markets is the risk element: the risk that share prices may fall or that they will choose the wrong stock, sector or region in which to invest. Hence, most people invest through collective investments and, indeed, collective investment funds of one sort or another hold most of the stock market values around the world. Being very large, funds can get good value for money on dealing fees, can spread their investments over a wide range of stocks while still being significant holders in most of the businesses in which they invest, have access to the services of investment analysts, economists and other legal and financial experts and employ professional managers, well trained in reaching a decision based on the

What most people fear about investing in stock markets is the risk element.

information available to have a better chance of being in the right place at the right time. However, even among collective investments, there are a number of different funds which serve a variety of purposes. It is not a part of this book's task to elaborate too far on the details of each type of fund as the law governing some key aspect of a particular fund type may change. However, an adviser will certainly be able to explain the differences in terms of your own requirements at the time. What follows is a brief and non-technical description of each.

Investment trusts

Investment trusts, although they are marketed as collective investments, are themselves companies whose sole assets are the shares of other companies. As such, investment trust shares are traded just like any others and they are susceptible to take-overs. Also, investment trusts are not open-ended in that they cannot simply create more shares to accommodate a new investor although new issues can be launched from time to time. The shares will have to be bought in the usual way. Investment trusts can borrow money to add value to the portfolio (gearing) which, if it is done shrewdly, will reap a return greater than the amount borrowed plus the cost of interest. However, borrowing to buy shares can have its downside if the shares fall in value or interest rates rise. The

Investment trust shares are traded just like any others.

directors of an investment trust are accountable to their shareholders as are the directors in any company. The value of an individual investment will reflect the underlying values of investments held by the investment trust adjusted by a factor to take account of the market's estimation of the prospects for the market and the quality of the investment management team. This will be reflected either as a discount to value, where the total value of shares is less than the value of assets held by the trust, or a premium over value where the total value of the trust's shares is greater than the value of its assets.

Unit trusts

More familiar to most people than investment trusts are unit trusts. In a unit trust, individual investments are pooled into a single fund which is divided into units. To arrive at a value for the units, the fund is invested in whatever assets fit the trust's criteria and those assets are priced to provide a value for the whole fund which, when divided by the number of units, provides the value of each unit. New investors may then join the fund by purchasing as many units as their investment will buy (subject to buying and selling charges). Unit trusts are true collective investments and are open-ended in that managers will, if necessary, issue new units to accommodate incoming investors. They have been around in the UK for some decades and underpin

In a unit trust, individual investments are pooled into a single fund which is divided into units.

the investment aspect of many other financial instruments, including insurance policies and pensions plans whose underlying funds often invest in unit trusts in order to spread their investments as widely as possible and to access the range of expertise present among the investment managers who run unit trusts. However, ordinary investors can also buy into unit trusts directly, either with a lump sum or regular savings. As an investor in a unit trust, you own a part of the fund and will see the value of your units rise or fall as the values of investments move.

OEICs

There is a new type of fund called an open-ended investment company (OEIC) to which a number of unit trust managers are switching. Without going into the full technicalities of them, OEICs are approved contracts in EU countries so that, unlike unit trusts which are operated to UK rules, OEICs can be marketed across

OEICs can be marketed across Europe.

Europe. This move towards OEICs was not particularly seismic at first but there was greater momentum in that direction during early 1999 in order to take advantage of the once and for all exemption from stamp duty for unit trusts switching to OEIC status before June 1999. Unit trusts or OEICs are probably the nearest to the stock market that most investors will get or would wish to get.

Insurance and pension plans

Probably the largest institutions through which most people invest are insurance and pensions providers. Insurance companies do not offer direct investments into their funds but, with the premiums you pay, they establish life funds from which they will be able to meet the liabilities under policies issued i.e. make payments at the time of a claim. In the past, where policyholders bought endowments, the company would value its investments each year, calculate by how much they had grown in value and allocate a portion of that growth to endowment policies as a bonus. Particularly in times of market growth, not all of the gain was passed to policyholders but what was not distributed went into a reserve from which bonuses could be supplemented in less good times. This made the endowment a very steady and predictable, if unexciting, saving and investment vehicle. In recent times, insurance companies have unitized their funds so that the returns earned by policyholders closely match the day-to-day fortunes of the fund. That is great in good times but, of course, values can go down as well as up!

Values can go down as well as up!

Pension funds are similar to insurance funds, often sharing an investment management team. However, pension funds operate under a different set of rules, partly to reflect the additional security that is needed when making provision for retirement income and partly to preclude abuse of the tax benefits available to those who save in a pension fund.

Friendly societies

Friendly societies are often confused with insurance companies and, indeed, they bear some corporate resemblance to that dwindling band of insurers who are constituted as mutual societies rather than companies. However, friendly societies are true mutuals and many still operate on the self-help principles that built the co-operative movement which is a large friendly society albeit with a range of operations and a fractured organizational structure. Many friendly societies were set up by trades unions so that those who had work and resources could support those less fortunate at a particular time. Because of their strong links with the Labour movement (not the party), friendly societies are natural for taking a socially responsible approach to investment but were, until recently, restricted in what they could offer. That problem was partly addressed by the 1992 Friendly Societies Act although the societies would like to go further than even that legislation allows and be able to compete on a level playing field with insurance societies and companies.

> *Friendly societies are true mutuals and many still operate on the self-help principles that built the co-operative movement.*

A vehicle to suit

There are a range of ways in which you may become an investor in the UK and there are a range of savings and investment vehicles to suit those different ways. There will be similar products available in most countries and, as regulations are harmonized to facilitate more open markets, the differences in structure from country to country will be eliminated. As with the funds, you would be best discussing your situation with a financial adviser before committing yourself to any particular plan. Although financial advisers have come in for some strong criticism in recent times, especially over the pensions mis-selling problem, as with any group, the newsworthy ones and their actions are not typical of a profession which has added great value to most of the people who have been advised on their financial planning over the years. Both the Ethical Investment Research Service (EIRIS) and the UK Social Investment Forum (UKSIF) maintain lists of independent financial advisers (IFAs) who will include a consideration of their client's ethical and environmental stance when advising on what investments are available.

Investing with a PEP

One of the most successful investment and savings plans of recent times has been the Personal Equity Plan (PEP). Offering considerable tax benefits in exchange for a commitment to invest rather than consume wealth, many people have built their saving programmes around

One of the most successful investment and savings plans of recent times has been the Personal Equity Plan (PEP).

the plan. Unfortunately, the current UK government has deemed PEPs not to be the right savings and investment vehicle for the future and have replaced them with a new product, the Individual Saving Account (ISA). Very few of the professionals in the financial planning industry regard ISAs as an adequate replacement for PEPs but there is no alternative. Within limits, investors will be able to hold shares or unit trust units in an ISA and that holding will be free of tax liabilities.

A good policy

Life insurance policies have always been a watchword for security and predictability. The deal is a good one. The policyholder pays a regular and relatively small sum to the insurer in return for which the insurer will pay out a large lump sum should the policyholder die during the term of the contract. Insurance policies come in all forms these days but the basic premise remains the same. However, because of the favourable tax treatment accorded to their funds and the fact that people are used to paying a regular amount to them, as well as the investment expertise that insurers deploy to maintain the ability of their life fund to meet liabilities, insurance policies have become good investments for those thinking long term.

Pension me off!

Pension plans are again very similar to insurance policies and are usually operated by the same organizations. The laws under which they operate are different but, for many people, saving for a retirement

income represents their largest commitment after the mortgage. So a pension
fund operating to socially accountable
rules would be a powerful force.

A pension fund operating to socially accountable rules would be a powerful force.

Be friendly

Again, we must not forget the savings plans of friendly societies which include tax-free products not available from other institutions and where ethical principles have long been a guiding force for investment managers.

Most importantly, all of the savings and investment vehicles and the different types of fund will include ethical and environmentally-aware choices which means that, if you care, you need not restrict yourself to a limited range of specialist opportunities.

A choice of funds

Having profiled your ideal fund using the pro-forma suggested in Figure 5.2 and having chosen an investment vehicle suitable to your circumstances and requirements, you will now wish to identify a group of funds which are managed to priorities similar to your own. You may write to a number of the fund managers listed at the end of this book to request a copy of the fund prospectus and, given the limited number of funds in existence today (*see* Chapter 9), it may even be practical to write to or telephone all of the fund managers. Using the prospectus, make a new copy of Figure 5.2 for each fund and complete the column which identifies your ideal fund. Then go through the same exercise for each fund under consideration to see which ones most closely match your ideal. There will, of course, be other factors that will need to be considered including past performance (not a guarantee of future performance but certainly an indicator), fund size, savings and investment vehicles available. Here, once again, the advice of an IFA will prove valuable.

If you would feel more comfortable using a more prescribed selection system, then invest in a copy of the EIRIS publication, 'Money and

Ethics' (a book in itself) which includes a comprehensive, step-by-step fund selector.

Knowledge is strength

In practice, the selection of a suitable ethical or environmental investment is much the same as selecting any suitable investment. The one exception is that, because the criteria by which concerned investors judge performance include some subjective elements, a little more time must be invested in understanding and prioritizing those elements. The advantage of this is that, just as socially accountable fund

The criteria by which concerned investors judge performance include some subjective elements.

managers know more about their investments as a result of their higher levels of research, so the individual investor will better understand his or her own feelings with the benefit of having had to evaluate them in this way.

Part 3

HOW THE PROFESSIONALS DO IT

Chapter 6

THE HISTORY AND CURRENT STATE OF AFFAIRS OF ETHICAL INVESTMENT

From noble origins to a concerted effort

The concept of ethical business practice is not new. In the New Testament of the Christian Bible, Jesus ejected the traders and money-changers from the precincts of the temple in Jerusalem, he was objecting not to their commerce, as such, but to their linking it with and trading on the emotions that people felt in a holy place. Indeed, the correct use of money is a recurring topic in New Testament teaching. Religious belief does not preclude building a successful and profitable business through hard work and enterprise but it should preclude achieving that end by unethical means. During the great industrialization and empire building period of the eighteenth and nineteenth centuries, many of the most successful commercial ventures were headed by families with strong religious commitment who believed in the value of hard work but who equally saw it as their responsibility, hand in hand with the running of the commercial enterprise, to ensure the welfare, comfort and spiritual fulfilment of those who worked in the organizations that they owned: hence the company towns, specified holidays, encouragement of music and reading that were established around the factories of the great businesses of their day. When the government today talks of stakeholders in a business, that concept is no more than a current expression of the way that commercial dynasties such as the Cadbury and Rowntree families always treated their personnel. So it is not surprising that the first efforts to include an ethical element into investment policies, probably in the 1920s, were by religious organizations or religiously inspired charities. And, of course, some religions did place particular emphasis on certain perceived sources of human undoing and misery. The Quakers are pacifists and so have always endeavoured to avoid any investment in the armaments industry or associated activities. As Methodists hold strong views as to the contributions of alcohol, tobacco and gambling to any impoverishment of the human condition, their investments have always avoided the industries that support and profit from those activities as well as the arms industry. Other churches followed similar lines and some began to expand the area of concern to include those newspapers whose output was deemed diminishing to human thought. In the 1960s, anti-war groups in American universities began to question the business ethics of companies who produced the materials used in war, such as Agent Orange, the defoliation chemical used to destroy potential ground cover in Vietnam. By the late 1960s and early 1970s, a number of organizations were including a moral dimension in their decisions as to where they might invest or which ventures they might support.

However, all of this worthiness could hardly be described as a movement or an investment criterion. It took a particular international political situation to provide a central issue around which those of an ethical turn of mind could gather their various efforts into a cohesive philosophy. That situation was South Africa and the horrible policy of apartheid or separate development which institutionalized the idea that one race was inferior to another because of difference in skin colour and culture. The issue caused a number of problems for UK and other investors with conscience. Many companies had built up strong links with and investments in South Africa in order to exploit that country's several values. It offered access to plentiful raw materials and, in particular, mineral deposits that included significant proportions of the world's gold and diamond resources. South Africa seemed well run, strongly policed and, a boon for businesses, it offered secure and reliable transport from the places where the minerals were extracted to equally well run ports, all supported by a strong military presence. This all contrasted very strongly with the apparent tribal chaos and instability that was making the rest of sub-Saharan, post-imperial Africa an increasingly inhospitable place to do business. Indeed, at one point, South African Railways and ports became the main means of getting most of the output of sub-Saharan Africa to markets in the developed world. However, the dark side to this story was that the stability and order were maintained with human repression on an appalling scale, made worse by the attitude that regarded black South Africans as a lesser race. In addition, some of the instability among South Africa's neighbours was instigated and fomented by agents of the white supremacists who ruled the southern part of the continent. The need to identify which businesses had links with South Africa and the extent of those links helped lay down the rules for assessing and screening the ethical and environmental aspects of potential investments which have remained, with increasing technical sophistication, to this day.

In the USA, churches and some state pension funds began to seek ways in which they could identify South African involvement by companies and, in the UK, two organizations established at this time, the Public Interest Research Centre (PIRC) and Christian Concern for Southern Africa (forerunner of the Ethical Investment Research Society) evolved the screening tools on which today's fund managers rely.

Pension power

At the same time that various churches were introducing an ethical stance to their investment policy, other groups were taking a similar route. Pension funds are among the most powerful investors of our day and the investment expectations of pension funds attached to large state organizations in government and in the wider economy can make a difference to the way businesses are run. However, even more than charities, the managers of pension funds have an obligation to achieve growth and income for their fundholders who would be unlikely to appreciate the ethics of an investment policy that diminished the quality of their retirement.

Russell Sparkes, fund manager of the Central Finance Board of the Methodist Church, has suggested that, in the UK, ethical funds associated with church investments amounted to at least £5 billion in 1998 and that 12–15 per cent of charity funds also applied ethical screening at that time which would account for a further £7 billion. In July 1997, EIRIS published a survey conducted among 52 well known charities which own company shares. Of the 52, 23 had formal ethical investment policies while a further 11 said that ethical concerns may influence their share-purchasing decisions. Another five were considering adopting ethical investment policies during the following year. Many local authority pension funds also apply some element of ethical screening as part of their stock selection procedure.

Many local authority pension funds also apply some element of ethical screening as part of their stock selection procedure.

A group effort

While churches, charities and some pension funds can muster very large sums of investment money, the really big hitters of the investment firmament are the companies who manage funds on behalf of other large numbers of investors, the group investment funds. Insurance companies, pension fund managers (often the same companies), unit trust managers and investment trusts control, according to some estimates, more than 85 per cent of the developed world's stock markets. In this sector, the process of incorporating a conscience into investment selection processes was a little more difficult.

When Charles Jacob, assisted by his fellow director at Vavasseur Unit Management, Jacob Edwards, and helped and financially supported by Richard Rowntree (through the Richard Rowntree Social Services Trust), first proposed the launch of the Stewardship Unit Trust in 1973, the licence was refused by the authorities of the day on the grounds that such a trust (if constrained to invest only in stocks which passed an ethical screening process) could not fulfil the obligation to seek the best possible return for investors which might, so the argument ran, be available from stocks, such as tobacco, alcohol or armaments producers, which could not pass such a screening process. When in 1976 Jacob and Edwards appealed against the Board of Trade decision, they were again refused on similar grounds. The value of persistence was illustrated, however, when two years later, Jacob enlisted the help of Sir Nicholas Goodison, then Chairman of the London Stock Exchange, and their approach finally met with an agreement in principle. Of course, only investors who wished such ethical criteria to be part of their fund's stock selection process would choose an ethical unit trust anyway but it was to take more than a decade from the initial proposal before, finally in 1984, approval was given to the first ethical fund under the auspices of Friends Provident. Interestingly, the concept was unchanged from the original stewardship proposal which had been turned down by the Board of Trade in 1973. The Stewardship Fund was the first vehicle through which ordinary investors could choose, with their eyes wide open and as a matter of principle, to invest in a manner which reflected their moral as well as their financial aspirations.

But ethical investors are not starry-eyed sentimentalists and to invest ethically is not the same as to try and change the whole world at once. Charles Jacob MBE, in his keynote speech to the October 1996 UKSIF General Meeting, told the story of 'an industrialist whose son was finding geography a difficult subject. So the father gave him a jigsaw puzzle of the world in the hope that this would enable the son to place the countries in their correct positions. The boy failed miserably to complete the picture, whereupon the father instructed him to turn over the jigsaw for there on the other side was a picture of his father standing outside the company building in which he worked – both so well known to the infant son. The picture and the puzzle were quickly completed.

Ethical investors are not starry-eyed sentimentalists.

'It is beyond our task to put the world right. We can only help by seeking to put the man and his company right in the hope that eventually the greater picture will be achieved. [Ethical investment] is not about platitudes – it is about attitudes!'

How the funds work

Ethical funds work in much the same way as any funds. They aim to maximize the growth and income from their investments so as to deliver the best possible return to investors but all within the requirement that stock selection should be within a particular universe of businesses which can be judged to operate ethically and in a manner

Ethical funds work in much the same way as any funds.

which does not damage the environment – businesses that grow and generate profit through adding real value in the process. That is really little different from selecting investments based on location or a particular industry or a stage in the development process i.e. from emerging markets or from natural resources or from UK small companies or from any other sector or area.

However, while it is relatively easy to establish whether a particular stock fits into one of the more usual categories, it takes a little more effort to establish ethical credentials. Each socially responsible fund has established and committed itself to a set of ethical and environmental criteria against which stocks will be measured. Sometimes in-house but more often using a screening service such as that provided by EIRIS, a fund manager will identify those companies whose operations meet the fund's criteria and that group of stocks (regularly updated) will form the pool of stocks from which the manager may purchase, subject to all of the usual management and financial criteria. Fund managers will still do all the things that other fund managers do, including visiting in person most, if not all, of the businesses whose stock is being considered for inclusion in the portfolio. In order to strengthen the process further, socially responsible funds are usually controlled by non-executive boards of people chosen for their expertise and knowledge in areas of ethical or environmental excellence.

Taking on more

There are limits to what fund managers can currently do. From an early position of avoiding investment in the shares of businesses whose

There are limits to what fund managers can currently do.

activities were not regarded as socially responsible or accountable, managers have moved on to a policy of investing in businesses whose activities are regarded as adding real and sustainable value to society in general and whose management approach is likely to fit them well for the social, legislative and opinion climate of the next century. This supportive process of positive selection might be summed up in the phrase used by Amnesty International: 'better to light a candle than to curse the darkness.' From this point, the plan becomes a little more confrontational and, although individuals and particular bodies in control of their own resources may go that far, managers responsible for the investment of other people's money may not yet be able to do so and will certainly not be able to do so using the funds available today.

The next stage in socially responsible investment is one where funds buy stocks in businesses of whose practices the fund managers disapprove. This, of course, is quite incompatible with the avoidance type of fund and cannot really be said to be in line with the support type of fund. However, this type of investment strategy is practised by churches and charities who would bring the force of their money and their argument right to the heart of a business, using their position as major shareholders to engage in a constructive dialogue. Along with the dialogue is the ever-present reality that a business which refused to take account of ethical views might find itself excluded from access to the growing pool of capital from ethical sources. It is debatable whether the terms under which any group investment operates could ever stretch so far as to accommodate this investment purpose. For individuals alone, there is the option of buying as few shares as are needed to attend a shareholders' meeting and, at that meeting, making a protest. This has proved effective as a means to draw public and shareholder attention to perceived social shortcomings in a company's operations but could not be regarded as an investment.

On the threshold of the future

Socially responsible, ethical, ecological or whatever type of investment you call it, investment with a conscience seems to be a movement in tune with the late 20th and early 21st century. However, not only was it an idea which would have been in tune with Christian teachings but

Investment with a conscience seems to be a movement in tune with the late 20th and early 21st century.

it also represents a philosophy familiar to many religions today. As John Wesley, the founder of Methodism and a renowned preacher, put it in the titles to four consecutive addresses delivered in the eighteenth century:

- *Gain all you can*
- *But not at the expense of your conscience*
- *Not at the expense of our neighbour's wealth*
- *Not at the expense of our neighbour's health.*

It could not have been put better.

Chapter 7

THE DILEMMAS OF AN ETHICAL INVESTMENT APPROACH

A mirror for changing values

In many senses, the movement towards more socially responsible investment has mirrored an opposite move in the world of collecting art and cultural artefacts. Legendary collections of past ages usually reflected, above all else, the tastes and passions of the collector. If a collection followed a theme, it was more likely to reflect how the owner felt about the objects of his or her aesthetic zeal than any purely objective view. Much of the value attributed to a collectable item lay in its appearance, provenance, feel or taste. Such collections were often put on display for the sheer joy of sharing a love for objects of perceived beauty or artefacts with a recognized place in history that had been accumulated and that, when viewed together, could bring to life a particular aspect of human achievement. In fact, wealthy collectors almost regarded it as a duty which came with their fortune (in both senses of the word) to share some of the qualities and values that fortune could acquire and thus to give back something to balance what they had taken. This was rarely motivated by any ethical concerns as we recognize them today but, nonetheless, did ensure that society as a whole was enriched. However, in the second half of the twentieth century, value had begun to be more closely defined as price. Collectors of this new school were still attracted to aesthetic qualities but equally or more concerned with previous form and performance in the price. Indeed, some 'collectors' were institutions such as pension funds rather than individuals at all and bought solely in the expectation of significant price rises. The passion was transferred from the object to its sale value and, because that was the guiding principle, many great works of art or other objects of significance disappeared into the safety of bank vaults. Individual collectors of this school took their pleasure from marking the rising tide of their particular market and, from that, assessing the value of their safely banked collections. Those were not pleasures to be shared. Institutional collectors regarded the objects as just more assets.

Institutional collectors regarded the objects as just more assets.

Investment into the stocks and shares of businesses, on the other hand, has traditionally always looked to the absolute value of price as its guiding light. Whether investing short term, long term, for income or for growth, the bottom line has been measured in terms of money. If any intuitive value was placed on an investment, it was more likely the speculation that it might outperform conventional expectations for monetary return or growth or the market sector in which it was categorized than any concern for the social, ethical, environmental or other human values that might be ascribed to the company or object in question. In many senses that made the management of group investment funds, if not easy, more predictable. The very fact that some investing institutions have programmed computers to buy or sell stocks according to specific trends, movements or trigger points in the price of shares is indicative of the absolute and quantifiable criteria by which investment value has traditionally been measured. In this tradition, there are a few definitions of what is a good investment. Will it make money this year? Will it make money next year? Will it make money into the foreseeable future? And will it beat inflation as well as other available investments in terms of the money it makes? All in all, there appears to be some foundation for a favourite phrase of the 1980s, that we have become a society which 'knows the price of everything while appreciating the value of nothing'.

We have become a society which 'knows the price of everything while appreciating the value of nothing'.

Investment with feeling and dilemmas

Ethical investment reflects a change in our perception of value. It has introduced into the valuation of investment values measured more in terms of decency and the cost to others of our profit. And, of course, socially responsible investors have pointed up the very real long-term financial cost of policies which pay no heed to issues beyond the immediate bottom line as well as the added financial value of policies which seek to run the business efficiently and in tune with the world at large. Socially responsible investors also recognize that a profit generated from true added value, without the need to exploit anybody, reflects the type of long-term business and management skills that will be more likely to thrive in good times as well as survive any bad times that the future may hold.

But that approach to investments is not without its difficulties. Apart from the need to research and monitor individual investments more closely than might always be the case for fund managers concerned primarily and nearly exclusively with bottom-line values, ethical fund managers have to deal with dilemmas – because ethical and environmental funds base their investment judgements on moral as well as statistical criteria. For this reason, there are almost as many definitions of a good investment as there are investors with ethical and environmental concerns! We have seen in earlier chapters the range of concerns that motivate some investors to consider the wider ramifications of a company's activities and more than simply the cost-effectiveness of its management. Those concerns are often very personal reflecting an individual's honestly and passionately held belief about what are the errors or values of human endeavour. Inevitably, those concerns cherished by one investor may well clash diametrically with the equally honestly and passionately held concerns of another. Such is human nature. Some would say that the presence of such dilemmas is a weakness in the drive to pursue a socially responsible investment policy. Others believe that it is the fact that such dilemmas exist that points to the thorough and considered approach upon which this particular investment movement is built and introduces the strength of real understanding into the investment equation. Also, in the course of resolving dilemmas, fund managers and investors alike may well improve the mechanisms by which they measure and judge the social aspects of an investment.

Dilemmas occur when two sincerely held and valid views on a particular issue lead to opposing conclusions.

Dilemmas occur when two sincerely held and valid views on a particular issue lead to opposing conclusions. As there are nearly as many ethical and environmental stances as there are concerned investors, it is inevitable that dilemmas will arise in the approach to some potential investments.

Perhaps yes, possibly no

An excellent example might be the seemingly straightforward matter of public transport. Here is an issue on which we can all agree, can we not? Companies who are developing and operating public transport services, infrastructure and equipment would appear to be good investments for a socially responsible fund manager. However, there have been a number of dilemmas around this issue and the manner in which these have been resolved offers some insight into the concerns of ethical funds: the realism with which they prioritize their concerns as well as the pragmatic approach which avoids unsound business activities or supports positive ones while at the same time seeking to use investment power to influence the direction and operation of the business.

Two companies in the forefront of the modern public transport system are Cowie Group and Stagecoach. Cowie is a major bus operator around the country but is also one of the UK's largest car dealerships. Dilemma: should the company be placed on the ethically acceptable list for taking people out of their cars or should it join the proscribed list for selling cars to those who still resist the charms of its public transport undertakings? The committee of reference whose members guide the Stewardship Fund at Friends Provident deliberated long and hard before deciding that 'on balance' Cowie should be an acceptable stock (not the same as deciding to buy it). Stagecoach posed a slightly different problem because the concerns were not about another part of its business, most of which is related to public transport (including buses and railways). The allegations were that the company had indulged in anti-competitive practices in its rise to become the UK's largest bus operator and about the conflicts of interest that might arise from Stagecoach's ownership of one of the train leasing businesses while being a significant train *Transport is a source of a number of dilemmas.* operator whose profitability is, at least partly, dependent on the cost of leasing trains. However, for some, the bottom line will be that buses and trains will help to take cars off the roads and an investment in the company will provide access to other investors and the opportunity to influence the decisions of the business. Indeed, transport is a source of a number of dilemmas.

Roads going where?

During the establishment of a route for the A30 road to bypass Fairmile in Devon, two quite different but equally sincerely held views were expressed. 'Building more roads encourages more travel . . . a short-term solution to a long-term problem. Of course I sympathise with people who are [currently] subjected to environmental pollution [from the overcrowded old road] but we must work towards [less vehicles on the roads and] more environmentally sound transport.' That was the view of one of the leading protestors, Daniel Hooper or 'Swampy', who, during protests aimed at preventing or delaying the scheme, occupied a tunnel under the site for the new road. But it was not the only view and certainly not the only sincerely held view.

The one-time landlady of the Fairmile Inn expressed the other side of the same story. 'The new road is necessary progress for the tourist industry, for trade, to maintain the local economy and for road safety. The volume of traffic would be difficult to appreciate unless you lived here. Any associated development would benefit the area. People want to go from A to B without going via C and D as public transport would.'

These two contrary but equally sincerely held views epitomize the type of dilemma faced by ethical and environmental fund managers.

Whose quality of life will be improved if a road is built and whose will be spoiled? There is evidence that new roads actually generate the growth in traffic levels that eventually choke them and lead to calls for yet more capacity. And yet, without an effective infrastructure, many of the manufacturing industries on which a large proportion of the population depend for their living will simply not move to an area or, if already there, may even move away to a more convenient and accessible place to accommodate future expansion plans (usually taking their jobs with them). There is no doubt that overseas companies seeking to locate in the UK will be very concerned as to what infrastructure is in place to support their operation and their proximity to that infrastructure. And if the road building programme is curtailed, as now seems to be the case under the Labour govern-

New roads actually generate the growth in traffic levels that eventually choke them.

ment, goods and people will still need to get around while, realistically, public transport and the railways, as currently structured, will not be able to take on the full load in the foreseeable future. One alternative being promoted is the use of technology to manage traffic flows but that also gives rise to a dilemma. Trafficmaster is a system that can direct drivers away from congestion and even suggest faster and less polluting alternatives but it requires a network of 5,000 infra-red sensors and 3,500 roadside beacons to gather and distribute its information. So will ethical fund managers avoid the businesses providing this service because their equipment is an eyesore? Or will they support the companies on the grounds that, as David Martell, chief executive of Trafficmaster, put it: 'In the absence of a comprehensive road building programme, technology can play a key role in helping to reduce both the cost and time wasted in congestion . . . and stress levels are significantly reduced.'?

But transport is not the only concern of ethical fund managers.

A complex judgement

Some will reflect a concern about how businesses treat their personnel, or the practices they deploy to advance the business; others will question the integrity of information used in marketing, or the fairness of any trading arrangements with countries from the developing world. Managers of funds which follow an environmental agenda can at least base their judgements on more measurable criteria – 'Does this company's activity harm the environment?' – although even that seemingly straightforward question can suggest different answers according to personal priorities. Whether the fund manager adheres to an ethical or environmental investment policy, there is an additional complication caused by the complex cross-ownership, joint ventures and other relationships of modern business. At first sight, the dilemmas faced by socially responsible investors can seem daunting.

However, since Friends Provident first launched the Stewardship Fund in 1984, ethical and environmental fund managers have worked towards refining the definitions which govern investment criteria from the avoidance-driven criteria of the protest movement to the more sophisticated supportive approach which seeks to promote good as well as avoid bad practices. As a result, cases such as the Cowie and Stagecoach examples can be considered not simply in terms of being against those activities considered environmentally or ethically poor but also in terms of how an investment might give the fund managers the opportunity, on behalf of their investors, to influence future development of policy in the business. Also, some previously avoided investments have matured or the conditions which defined their status have lost that edge which gives rise to outrage in some investors. That, though, takes managers into difficult areas and there are now a number of investment propositions with strong arguments both for and against them on ethical and environmental grounds. Avoidance criteria still outnumber support criteria by eighteen to five in the 1998 edition of the EIRIS report, 'Money and Ethics' and that, combined with the dilemmas that ethical and environmental investment can encounter could deter some investors

It would not be socially responsible or, indeed, ethical to throw investors' money into businesses with little hope of success.

from making the effort to establish which fund might share their priorities. It should not do so because, for an investor who is concerned about the wider issues, it is these dilemmas and the reasoning which goes into resolving them that give ethical investment its human edge. And remember, while socially responsible fund managers do include ethical and environmental criteria in their considerations, they are still obliged to achieve the best financial performance they can within those parameters. As stated in Chapter 1, it would not be socially responsible or, indeed, ethical to throw investors' money into businesses with little hope of success.

Understanding from a reference to knowledge

The resolution of dilemmas is best achieved through the application of information which is a task that EIRIS (the Ethical Investment Research Service) undertakes for those funds who retain the service as an adviser and for investors who subscribe for the regularly updated research which supports its findings. EIRIS is retained as an adviser by 18 fund managers (1998 report) to provide what might be described as a clarifying service. Without expressing opinions of its own, EIRIS analyzes and reports on companies in terms of established and agreed ethical and environmental criteria and the specific criteria which each fund has proclaimed as its own. Managers may then use this information as a first filter against the fund's own policy before applying the usual research and financial examinations. EIRIS does, though, encourage funds to have a clear investment policy on ethical and environmental issues because it is only through such a policy that fund managers can make clear their own criteria to potential investors in such terms as will enable those investors to determine whether or not the fund stands on their general side of a dilemma. Some fund managers will also refer to ethical reference committees, independent bodies who adjudicate on whether a potential investment is within or outside an acceptable level of compliance with the policy of the fund. However, for all of the general agreement between a fund and its fund holders as far as priorities are concerned, there will be specific issues that either fall outside previous understandings as to the criteria or which break new ground for which no clear criteria had been established when the fund holder first invested.

Good guy, bad guy

In order to cater continually for the diversity in approach of different ethical investors and their advisers, as well as the dilemmas that can arise from those differences, some fund managers, NPI for instance, operate parallel investment policies. 'Global Care Unit Trust and Pensions Global Care,' explained a spokesperson for NPI, 'adhere to strict avoidance criteria whereas Global Care Income Unit Trust and Pensions Global Care Managed Fund are overall support-orientated funds, looking to the future and taking a realistic stance.'

'The first investment sector that comes to mind when speaking of dilemmas would be armaments,' in the view of Mike Shaw, Chief Executive at NPI Global Care Investments. Who, for instance, arms the peacemakers? You may dislike arms and the trade which spreads them around the world but, if you support the principle of peace-keeping, the peace-keepers must be able to defend themselves against the attacks that are all too likely in any place where the peace needs to be kept. If a force is required to keep peace then the underlying situation must be one of conflict. Without their arms, peace-keepers cannot so effectively maintain order. It may appear to be a dilemma but socially responsible investors will look beyond the immediate reaction and consider the full case. Operating two funds enables the managers to cater for both sides of the dilemma in this and other areas.

Arms linkages are, like transport issues, often the cause of dilemmas – and not only for investors and fund managers. Events in Sierra Leone during 1998 posed, for the British government, the dilemma of whether it had been right to arm the forces of the democratically elected but ousted government in order to assist in the overthrow of the unelected and unpleasant regime that had seized power in the country. Had a strict definition of ethical foreign policy been observed, no arms would have been supplied but the people of Sierra Leone would have had to live for an indefinite period under the oppressive yoke of a government that operated to particularly barbaric standards. On balance and regardless of the political issues, the forward-looking observer would say that the decision to assist the elected government with arms to overthrow the unelected dictators was morally correct, whatever the legal position. Often, though, the dilemmas faced by ethical investors are much less global.

The case for defence

For instance, in the UK, a company called RPS (Rural Planning Services) had always enjoyed a clean bill of health on its environmental activities. Although sometimes involved in preparing development plans, the business was generally perceived as being sensitive to environmental matters. Then RPS won a Ministry of Defence contract to clear former training areas and restore them as closely as possible to the condition in which the army had found them when it moved in. That link with the MoD lost the business its place on most lists of ethically approved investments because funds, on behalf of their investors, would avoid any business with MoD contracts, as a matter of policy. But the contract was to undertake an environmentally positive restoration programme and might be said to be contributing to, or at least supporting, a reduction in the armed forces. Environmental fund managers could well find the investment acceptable and ethical managers should also be able to argue a case for investment.

Trinity Holdings manufacture Dennis public service vehicles, buses, fire engines and refuse trucks – all vehicles for very positive public service purposes and environmentally sound. The company was regarded as a socially responsible investment until it won a contract to build two special handling vehicles to be used by the Ministry of Defence for unloading returning Army of the Rhine tanks from the ships which had transported them from Germany, prior to their transfer to barracks where they would be decommissioned. There was then what might best be described as a knee-jerk reaction to an involvement with the MoD until some had considered the matter in full and decided that, on balance, Trinity was still OK; it was, after all, contributing to an overall reduction in armaments.

Because armaments are such heavy users of design, development, manufacturing and assembly capabilities, arms seem to get into all sorts of linkages. At first sight you may consider a company that develops wind power generators to be, indisputably, a socially responsible investment but one such developer is Boeing, one of the USA's three dominant builders of military aircraft and equipment. However, Boeing also builds passenger aircraft, including long-haul, efficient, two-engine machines which create less pollution per passenger mile than older types of aircraft. This particular dilemma grows more complex when one considers also that, 'While wind power generation is seen as a good idea by some, that view is definitely not shared by those who find themselves living near to the very large windmills and their 24-hour drone.' Richard Singleton of Friends Provident adds more pieces to the puzzle. And as a final matter for thought, many of the wind powered turbines used in the UK are owned by National Power, one of the country's largest producers of greenhouse gases!

Of course, many of those greenhouse gases are a by-product from the burning of fossil fuels including coal which, in the UK, is mined mainly by RJB Mining, the company that bought most of the assets of British Coal at privatization. The dilemma for fund managers is that, while RJB's environmental case may be difficult to establish, the company has maintained, through direct employment in its mines and indirect employment in the places where miners live, communities which might otherwise have died. RJB is also involved in the development of a Clean Coal Power Station which may be a more pragmatic and realistic option for power generation, at least in the short to medium term.

Waste not . . .

Waste management is a growing business sector and investment area. But even here, caution must be a watchword as one senior researcher with the Environment Research Unit at Jupiter Asset Management explained, 'Waste management is widely perceived as being environmentally friendly but there are still problems such as leakage. We look for companies moving up the hierarchy of waste management, towards materials recovery . . . and away from pure disposal.' Such a business might be Philip Environmental, a Canadian business which has made significant

Waste management is a growing business sector and investment area.

advances in recycling as opposed to disposal, as has the Waste Recycling Company in the UK. But how would fund managers view a company like Nyrex which disposes (safely, we hope) of radioactive waste which cannot be recycled? No dilemma there as yet; most funds will avoid any business involved in the nuclear industry. But for how long? After all, nobody would contend that we would be better off without their activities in the safe disposal of materials that, whether we like them or not, do exist and must be safely managed for the foreseeable future.

Murky political waters

Of course, politics can influence views as to what is ethical or not and, for some, that simple device avoids many dilemmas. For instance, when the magazine *Ethical Consumer* announced that one of the ethical investment funds held shares in the *Daily Mail* group (no condemnation but the inference was clear) it may have overlooked the fact that the *Daily Mirror* had more advertising complaints found against it than the *Mail*. Many ethical fund managers would consider any press involvement good in that it informs and provides a forum for public debate, all at an affordable price.

Politics can influence views as to what is ethical or not.

Political perceptions can also change with the force of events as when considering South Africa. During the time of apartheid, socially responsible investment managers deliberately eschewed investments in the country as part of the pressure to bring about the end of apartheid. The same managers may now view involvement in the reborn state as positive support for a regime facing many problems whose solution will depend on the speed of economic and business development. However, others continue to steer clear on financial and value grounds. African countries have a poor track record of success with democracy, human rights or development and South Africa offers few reasons to suspect that it may be different. Also, there remain income disparities between most white and most black workers doing comparable jobs. Perhaps this is a dilemma that some would prefer to address based on faith rather than fact. It is certainly one which will challenge the decision-making powers of managers whose commitment to do their best with other people's money precludes placing that money anywhere they perceive to be financially uncertain.

One other area has seen political views sometimes muddy the waters of reasoned consideration and give rise to dilemmas. Many ethical investors opposed the privatization of state-owned industries. But times change and most privatized businesses have established strong environmental and ethical credentials, politics aside. British Telecom operates a service which contributes a real plus to the environment (telephone calls, video-conferences and the like reduce the need for travel) which is one reason why BT stock appears in more socially responsible portfolios than any other. The business also sets an example in the

Most privatized businesses have established strong environmental and ethical credentials.

openness with which it addresses environmental and ethical matters through an environmental unit which is about to embark on annual sustainability audits detailing, among other things, the plans for and actual disposal of all spent materials – from wire to lorries. The only concern that ethical fund managers may harbour about BT would be its involvement in communications systems that can have military applications.

Other former state-owned businesses have had fluctuating fortunes in this area. British Airways, it was said at the time of privatization, would become the pantomime horse of the airline industry. It has grown into the world's most successful airline. The airline's handling of redundancies was regarded as being of a good quality and so BA would have become an ethical choice but for the small matter of taking a rival's passengers. That is now receding into the past but, for fund managers following an ethical course, the dilemma remains. Environmental fund managers would, however, not be so concerned. Railtrack, on the other hand, is a recent privatization and to support environmentally sound transport systems but not Railtrack could easily lead to the question, at least as far as physical movement is concerned, 'If not railways, what?'

The Railtrack issue is an example of how dilemmas can foster better communications between fund managers, their investors and investments. When NPI Global Care Investments was considering whether to add Railtrack to the list of approved investments for the fund, managers wrote to investors. The Position Paper sent to unit holders was a good example of a realistic and apolitical attitude towards properly privatized enterprises and illustrates the lengths to which some fund managers will go to ensure that ethical and environmental credentials are exercised based on informed decisions, as the Paper's treatment of privatization shows.

'[Privatization] . . . is a fact we cannot stop . . . It is from this starting point that we must consider our best option . . . We now believe the most appropriate course is to invest and use our position as concerned shareholders to influence future decisions and priorities. Even groups like Transport 2000, who are opposed to privatization, nonetheless agree that . . . it will be important to hold Railtrack to the commitments they have made.' Given the facts, the majority of investors agreed but the exercise added strength to the decision and was in keeping with the informed and thoughtful nature of this type of investment. A good example of how the way in which a dilemma was handled actually strengthened the final investment decision.

A case for feelings

Lastly, there are the very emotional issues which can raise passions on both sides of the argument. Most ethical investors would wish to avoid companies who used animals as subjects of experiments or for testing new products prior to their use on people. However, there is a contrary view that says that use of animals is acceptable if the purpose is to achieve an advance in one of the sciences associated with health care and improving the condition of the human race. While funds which take that view would be able to invest in a business seeking a cure for cancer or other life-threatening conditions even where the search for a cure used animal experiments, the fund managers would, on behalf of their investors, always wish to be assured of the humanitarian care taken by the company and no fund will invest in a company that tests cosmetics on animals. But even that once included an apparent dilemma because most governments insisted that new cosmetic ingredients were first tested on live specimens. In that case, the only alternative was to halt any further cosmetic developments until a way could be found to test on volunteer humans and that is precisely the course that some manufacturers take although not with wholly new preparations. In late 1998, the UK government reached an agreement with the three remaining holders of licences for testing cosmetics on animals that the companies concerned would not reapply for those licences.

One emotive medical issue on which different people hold diametrically opposed but principled views is that of abortion. Because many of those who first looked to the ethical content of an investment did so from a religious belief, there was an emphasis on the sanctity of human life, including the life of the unborn child. However, those who are now taking the ethical road may well believe that a woman's right to choose is the overriding consideration when an abortion is considered.

> *Fund managers may have to consider offering a choice of ethical criteria in different funds.*

Fund managers will have to think hard on that one and may have to consider offering a choice of ethical criteria in different funds.

Another emotive issue is that of child labour but, again, it is not straightforward. While to our first world eyes, the employment of children as young as five to operate processes or sew garments may seem barbaric, when that work is halted, how will the families of the children replace the income? Sometimes, it is not enough simply to avoid what we do not like. We must also support a means to develop an alternative, such as improved education facilities and fairer trade for an industry which employs older people.

> *Sometimes, it is not enough simply to avoid what we do not like. We must also support a means to develop an alternative.*

Communications

In their relationships with companies in which they have invested, socially responsible investment managers operate in much the same way as most investors with, perhaps, the addition that some managers will tell a company if their shares are being sold because of a deterioration in their ethical or environmental score. And it works both ways. The store group, Kingfisher, for instance, informed environmental fund managers when the company adopted a policy of offering only products containing wood from renewable sources. With the ethical investment market growing rapidly, why would a company wish to exclude itself from the opportunity to attract such funds?

Many dilemmas are resolved through fund managers asking their own committee of reference or ethical board to establish guidelines as to what may or, on balance, may not be considered acceptable within the stated ethical and/or environmental criteria adopted by the fund. For instance, as in the case of the A30 extension and the Newbury Bypass, road projects may well face the problem of emotions receiving more exposure than facts. To avoid this problem, Friends Provident asked its Ethical Committee of Reference to develop guidelines against which road builders may be judged. That role of the independent committees is important to a majority of funds. John Whitney, chairman of the committee of reference for Stewardship Funds at Friends Provident explained, 'The process that the committee of reference brings to fund management is one that combines the resource and intelligence of EIRIS [an independent analyst] and the independent ethical stance of committee members who contribute a wide range of knowledge and experience.'

Insurance and banking

The financial sector generally gives rise to a number of dilemmas for ethical investors. Although the services offered by businesses in this sector are, of themselves, clean (indeed insurance is a laudable bulwark against some of life's worst events), the investments which support them are not universally subject to ethical or environmental screening.

Fund managers would argue that without the investment policies they use, they could not attract sufficient funds from across the investment universe to make their service work financially. Others would argue that, in making funds available to companies and regimes (strong bank loans) whose ethical and environmental records are questionable, insurance companies and banks are effectively turning a blind eye and helping to delay any change for the better.

Life is rarely simple, so why should investment be so?

There are dilemmas, yes, but dilemmas that are addressed by socially responsible fund managers and dilemmas whose demands for research make those fund managers better informed about the individual companies in which they invest. And the presence of dilemmas is not something which could be thought of as exclusive to socially responsible investment. Life very rarely offers simple choices although we sometimes exclude the difficult ones for the sake of a quick decision. The dilemmas of socially responsible investment and the manner in which they are addressed add to the analysis and understanding of the issues in question. While the choice may sometimes include more than a pinch of pragmatism, it may be better to invest in a business that, on balance, will add value to life on earth than to continue to the holy grail of the perfect socially responsible business. In investment as in life, if you want more out, you must put more in. For ethical investors, this means more thought about what they really wish to avoid, support or achieve with their investment.

Part 4

CURRENT AND FUTURE OUTLOOK FOR CONCERNED INVESTMENT

Chapter 8

THE IMPACT OF 'GREEN' INVESTMENT

Business first – get the message!

The theme throughout this book is that ordinary investors, whether through involvement with group investments or directly by buying shares in businesses of which they approve or in the running of which they would like to have a say, can send a message to organizations with the power to make a difference. You should know by now the message you wish to communicate, whether you wish to send that message and how to send it. However, it is one thing to send a message; the real question is, will it be received and will the recipients do anything about it? Then the further question arises: are those recipients in a position to make any difference or are they simply small, insignificant or ideologically motivated organizations that, whatever they decide to do, can make no difference to actions and activities in the real world? These are very important questions because the answers will determine whether socially responsible business practices are to be condemned to linger on the fringe of the real world, well regarded but largely ignored, or whether they might eventually become the standards and protocols for the conduct of all businesses. In order for that to be the case, the ranks of companies practising social responsibility will need to cover the full spectrum from service providers to manufacturers, from small specialist new ventures to large established, respected and successful businesses, from local enterprises to multinational conglomerates. In fact, the recruitment of large and successful businesses to the ranks of those

> *It is one thing to send a message; the real question is, will it be received and will the recipients do anything about it?*

who regard decency, integrity and environmental responsibility as integral to good business practice will be essential to the long-term success of the socially responsible agenda. And the news on that front is good.

Ethical business, not cottage industry

In April 1997, Tim Melville-Ross, director general at the Institute of Directors, told business leaders that, unless they recognized and dealt with their ethical responsibilities, 'business is in danger of losing its licence to operate and failing to deliver growth and prosperity.' Following this line of thought, the December 1997 issue of *Financial Director* magazine published a list of companies whose shares are held by three or more ethical funds. These are companies that meet the two key socially accountable investment standards: they are good business practices and are considered a worthwhile investment. Position on this list or absence from it does not necessarily indicate a failure to meet socially accountable standards and, because the list was drawn up in late 1997, some companies will have joined the list and others may have left since the survey. Also, the number of funds who hold some shares in a business is not the same as the number of shares held by socially accountable funds. However, caveats aside, Table 8.1 provides an interesting and encouraging insight into the impact of socially accountable investment on the principles and practices of business. That the survey was conducted by a magazine whose readers hold the corporate purse strings and are not noted for their sentimental approach to the job, suggests a sea change is taking place in the attitude of businesses towards the value of including social responsibility criteria in the running of a company.

Some points stand out in this list. First of all, the company whose shares are held by most ethical and environmental funds is British Telecom; no cottage industry, that! But what other means of communication could more effectively reduce the use of cars and even of public transport while maintaining the necessary lines of contact on which business is built? Then it is interesting to see how many of the companies listed are mainstream, large and successful businesses. And

Table 8.1
THE UK'S TOP ETHICAL COMPANIES

Number of ethical funds investing in company

Company	1	2	3	4	5	6	7	8	9	10	11	12	13
British Telecom *(telecoms)*	1	3	4	9	14	18	19	20	21	22	25	27	29
British Polythene Inds *(paper, p&p)*	2	3	4	7	9	14	16	17	19	20	22	23	
Railtrack *(trans)*	2	3	9	11	14	16	20	21	22	23	24	29	
Body Shop Int'l *(retail)*	1	3	4	9	14	16	17	21	22	27	28		
Wessex Water *(water)*	1	2	3	4	10	14	20	22	23	27	30		
Abbey National *(banks*	2	3	6	11	13	14	17	18	21	22			
Halma *(engineering)*	3	4	5	8	11	14	16	17	27	28			
Powerscreen Int'l *(engineering)*	2	3	4	5	6	8	17	19	20	28			
RPS Grp *(services)*	1	8	9	11	19	20	22	23	24	29			
SIG *(build m&m)*	3	4	14	16	17	20	22	23	24	25			
Biocompatibles Int'l *(health)*	3	10	12	19	20	27	28	29	30				
Polypipe *(build m&m)*	3	4	7	14	16	17	26	27	30				
Protean *(engineering)*	4	8	9	17	20	22	23	24	27				
Berkeley Grp *(bldg&cons)*	7	14	16	17	22	26	27	30					
Enterprise Oil *(oil e&p)*	3	13	14	15	16	26	29	30					
Greenway Hldgs *(services)*	4	8	9	17	19	20	22	27					
Marks & Spencer *(retail)*	1	3	7	9	14	16	17	30					
Persimmon *(bldg&cons)*	13	14	15	16	17	22	23	29					
Reuters *(media)*	3	9	14	22	23	24	25	29					
Safeway *(food retail)*	1	3	4	14	15	21	22	30					
Severn Trent *(water)*	3	6	8	11	20	21	22	26					
Tesco *(food retail)*	3	4	7	9	17	21	30						
Bank of Scotland *(banks)*	1	2	7	9	11	27	30						
Cable & Wireless *(telecoms)*	1	14	18	21	22	23	29						
Capital Radio *(media)*	7	14	16	17	22	23	27						
Care First Grp *(health)*	1	4	10	16	22	23	26						
Celsis Int'l *(health)*	1	7	19	22	23	27	28						
FirstBus *(trans)*	1	7	18	20	22	23	30						
Land Securities *(media)*	2	7	9	14	15	16	17						
Menvier-Swain Grp *(electronics)*	4	7	9	14	16	26	29						
Next *(retail)*	2	3	7	14	16	17	29						
Reed Int'l *(media)*	2	4	7	11	17	22	23						
Trinity Int'l *(media)*	3	7	14	16	17	26	27						
Waste Recycling Grp *(services)*	2	8	17	19	20	22	23						
City Technology Hldgs *(chem)*	2	6	7	16	26	28							
Cranswick *(food producers)*	1	2	17	19	20	22							
Eurocamp *(leisure)*	15	16	17	19	20	22							

1 Fund reference number (see Table 11.1)

Table 8.1 *cont.*

Number of ethical funds investing in company

	1	2	3	4	5	6	7	8	9	10	11	12	13
Eurotherm *(electronics)*	4	6	14	16	18	19							
Forth Ports *(trans)*	2	11	14	16	17	26							
Glaxo Wellcome *(pharm)*	1	3	4	9	14	29							
Hozelock Grp *(leisure)*	3	7	11	16	17	26							
Intercare Grp *(health)*	1	4	15	16	19	20							
Kingfisher *(retail)*	4	14	16	19	22	27							
Pearson *(media)*	4	7	14	17	18	25							
Prudential Corp *(life assur)*	2	7	9	11	29	30							
Recycling Services Grp *(services)*	2	8	15	16	19	20							
Smith (David S) *(paper, p&p)*	3	4	9	17	21	26							
Airtours *(leisure)*	1	11	14	16	29								
Anglian Grp *(build m&m)*	15	17	20	22	26								
ASDA *(food retail)*	7	9	14	17	27								
Ashtead Grp *(bldg&cans)*	11	16	17	26	30								
BG *(gas)*	3	4	10	22	26								
British Biotech *(pharm)*	3	7	18	27	29								
Corporate Services Grp *(services)*	3	4	22	23	27								
Creighton's Naturally *(household)*	1	15	19	20	26								
CRT Grp *(services)*	4	14	16	22	23								
Dixons Grp *(retail)*	3	11	17	21	29								
EMI Grp *(media)*	2	14	18	29	30								
General Accident *(insurance)*	9	22	23	25	29								
Go-Ahead Grp *(trans)*	16	19	20	22	23								
Johnson Grp Cleaners *(services)*	3	4	15	16	26								
Johnson Matthey *(engineering)*	4	8	10	14	21								
National Express *(trans)*	14	16	17	22	23								
Nestor Healthcare Grp *(health)*	4	7	19	20	26								
Orange *(telecoms)*	19	22	23	24	25								
RM *(services)*	16	22	23	24	26								
Rolfe & Nolan *(services)*	2	7	14	16	18								
Rubicon Grp *(engineering)*	4	7	14	15	16								
Scotia Hldgs *(pharm)*	1	4	22	27	29								
Servomex *(electronics)*	4	7	8	16	23								
Spirax-Sarco *(engineering)*	8	17	19	22	23								
Thorn *(retail)*	7	17	19	20	30								
Tunstall Grp *(electronics)*	4	7	14	16	28								
Visual Action Hldgs *(media)*	7	11	16	22	26								
Whatman *(engineering)*	8	16	17	19	20								
WPP Grp *(media)*	14	18	21	26	29								

Table 8.1 *cont.*

Number of ethical funds investing in company

	1	2	3	4	5	6	7	8	9	10	11	12	13
Alexandra Workwear *(textiles)*	1	14	15	16									
Allied Carpets *(retail)*	14	16	26	30									
Anglian Water *(water)*	2	4	9	10									
Avesco *(media)*	7	14	16	30									
Barbour Index *(media)*	7	15	16	27									
Barratt Developments *(bldg&cons)*	9	15	16	26									
Bath Press Grp *(paper, p&p)*	19	20	22	23									
Bellway *(bldg&cons)*	16	17	22	23									
Blue Circle Inds *(build m&m)*	7	9	21	26									
British-Borneo Petroleum *(oil e&p)*	14	16	26	29									
BTG *(services)*	22	23	24	29									
Burford Hldgs *(property)*	14	16	29	30									
Cairn Energy *(oil e&p)*	6	14	16	29									
Carlton Communications *(media)*	1	2	16	17									
Carpetright *(retail)*	14	16	27	30									
Celltech *(pharm)*	3	12	27	30									
Chiroscience Grp *(pharm)*	1	7	12	27									
Claremont Garments *(text)*	14	15	16	17									
Coutts Consulting Grp *(services)*	14	15	16	30									
Cowie Grp *(trans)*	11	14	16	30									
Crestcare *(health)*	1	7	10	30									
Dorling Kindersley *(media)*	3	16	26	27									
EMAP *(media)*	4	7	14	16									
First Technology *(engineering: vehicles)*	4	5	21	27									
Granada Grp *(leisure)*	9	14	21	29									
Great Portland Estates (b) *(property)*	3	14	16	30									
Iceland *(food retail)*	3	17	19	20									
Kwik-Fit Hldgs *(distribution: vehicles)*	3	4	14	16									
Lloyds TSB Grp *(banks)*	9	14	18	29									
Low & Bonar *(paper p&p)*	7	22	23	24									
Mackie Int'l Grp *(engineering)*	1	7	19	20									
Manchester United *(leisure)*	11	14	16	22									
Medeva *(pharm)*	4	18	29	30									
Mentmore Abbey *(services)*	5	7	14	16									
More Grp *(media)*	11	14	16	26									
MSB Int'l *(services)*	14	16	27	30									
Porvair *(chem)*	7	9	16	27									
Provident Financial *(financial)*	2	3	7	9									
Rotork *(engineering)*	4	5	8	28									

Table 8.1 *cont.*

Number of ethical funds investing in company

	1	2	3	4	5	6	7	8	9	10	11	12	13
The Sage Grp *(services)*	7	11	26	29									
Shanks & McEwan Grp *(services)*	3	19	20	29									
Smith & Nephew *(health)*	4	10	14	30									
St Ives *(paper, p&p)*	7	14	16	26									
Standard Chartered *(banks)*	9	11	18	29									
Storehouse *(retail)*	3	7	22	23									
Sutcliffe, Speakman *(chem)*	19	20	22	23									
Time Products *(distribution)*	11	26	27	30									
TLG *(electronics)*	3	15	16	20									
Treatt *(food)*	5	19	20	23									
Vision Grp *(electronics)*	7	18	19	26									
Vodafone Grp *(telecoms)*	4	9	17	21									
Alliance & Leicester *(banks)*	18	21	22										
Ash & Lacy *(engineering)*	13	15	16										
Barclays *(banks)*	9	18	29										
Beazer Grp *(bldg&cons)*	15	16	26										
Black (Peter) Hldgs *(household)*	4	7	26										
Blick *(electronics)*	4	14	16										
BPB *(build m&m)*	4	7	14										
BPP Hldgs *(services)*	3	4	16										
Bradford Property Trust *(property)*	2	14	16										
Britannic Assurance *(life assur)*	11	18	21										
Brunner Mond *(chem)*	14	15	16										
Calluna *(electronics)*	18	19	20										
Capital Shopping Centres *(property)*	1	15	16										
Centrica *(gas)*	3	4	10										
Compass Grp *(brew, pub & rest)*	7	17	30										
Cortecs Int'l *(pharm)*	1	3	27										
Croda Int'l *(chem)*	9	11	28										
Dart Grp *(trans)*	15	16	27										
Development Securities *(property)*	14	16	30										
Ellis & Everard *(chem)*	14	16	26										
Fl Grp *(services)*	7	11	26										
Fitness First *(leisure)*	14	15	16										
Frogmore Estates *(property)*	14	15	16										
Gall Thomson Environmental *(oil e&p)*	17	19	29										
Geest *(food producers)*	3	17	27										
Grantchester Hldgs *(property)*	16	26	30										
Guardian Royal Exchange *(insurance)*	2	18	30										

Table 8.1 *cont.*

Number of ethical funds investing in company

	1	2	3	4	5	6	7	8	9	10	11	12	13
Hardy Oil & Gas *(oil e&p)*	14	16	26										
Harris (Philip) *(distribution)*	4	7	22										
Harvey Nash Grp *(services)*	16	26	30										
Hays *(services)*	7	14	29										
Headlam Grp *(distribution)*	14	15	16										
Healthcall Grp *(health)*	15	16	17										
Hemingway Properties *(property)*	14	15	16										
Hewden-Stuart *(bldg&cons)*	7	14	16										
HSBC Hldgs *(banks)*	9	18	29										
Huntleigh Technology *(health)*	7	16	27										
Hyder *(water)*	8	21	28										
Industrial Control Services *(electronics)*	7	15	16										
Innovative Technologies *(health)*	7	18	27										
ISA Int'l *(distribution)*	14	16	17										
Jarvis *(bldg&cons)*	22	23	26										
JJB Sports *(retail)*	2	14	16										
Legal & General *(life assur)*	2	3	7										
Leigh Interests *(services)*	1	2	28										
Litho Supplies *(distribution)*	14	15	16										
London & Manchester Grp *(insurance)*	18	22	23										
Lorien *(services)*	16	22	23										
MEPC *(property)*	2	14	16										
Mercury Asset Management *(financial)*	2	11	21										
MFI Furniture Grp *(retail)*	9	26	29										
Millennium & Copthorne Hotels *(leisure)*	7	14	16										
Misys *(services)*	1	29	30										
Monument Oil and Gas *(oil e&p)*	14	16	27										
National Grid *(electricity)*	9	14	30										
NatWest Bank *(banks)*	18	22	25										
Northern Ireland Electricity *(electricity)*	2	4	11										
Nottingham Grp Hldgs *(retail)*	3	15	16										
Nursing Home Properties *(property)*	7	15	22										
Oliver Ashworth Grp *(distribution)*	4	15	16										
Orbis *(services)*	14	16	30										
Peek *(electronics)*	4	19	28										
Pilkington *(build m&m)*	19	22	21										
Pressac Hldgs *(electronics)*	7	11	26										
PSD Grp *(services)*	16	22	23										
Queens Moat Houses *(leisure)*	3	14	16										

Table 8.1 *cont.*

Number of ethical funds investing in company

	1	2	3	4	5	6	7	8	9	10	11	12	13
RPC Grp *(paper, p&p)*	7	16	26										
Ruberoid *(build m&m)*	15	16	17										
Sainsbury (J) *(food retail)*	4	14	22										
Scottish Media *(media)*	7	16	18										
Scottish Power *(electricity)*	4	21	26										
Shire Pharmaceuticals Grp *(pharm)*	1	7	30										
Smith (WH) Grp *(retail)*	3	9	30										
Streamline Hldgs *(build m&m)*	15	16	26										
Swallowfield *(household)*	3	19	20										
Tandem Grp *(leisure)*	3	19	20										
TBI *(property)*	14	16	30										
Tinsley Robor *(paper, p&p)*	2	11	22										
Tops Estates *(property)*	15	16	17										
Trafficmaster *(trans)*	26	27	30										
UniChem *(health)*	1	4	17										
United Assurance Grp *(life assur)*	2	18	30										
VCI *(leisure)*	7	15	16										
Wace Grp *(paper, p&p)*	7	15	16										
Waste Management Int'l *(services)*	4	10	29										
Watmoughs (Hldgs) *(paper, p&p)*	14	16	23										
Wilson Bowden *(bldg&cons)*	14	16	27										
Wiseman (Robert) Dairies *(food producers)*	14	16	30										
Wyevale Garden Centres *(retail)*	6	15	27										

This information is taken from the latest available manager's/annual reports.

There are two criteria for ethical investments: a company must satisfy certain ethical thresholds set by fund managers and its shares must be considered to be a worthwhile investment.

Positioning on this list or absence from it does not necessarily indicate a failure to meet ethical standards.

Source: Copyright *Financial Director*, December 1997.

the spread of sectors includes most mainstream business activities. So, it would appear to be quite possible to operate a successful business of any size in a mainline sector of economic activity while maintaining decent, honest standards that take account of the business's impact on people, the environment and long-term outcomes.

How could you tell?

But how would a business know whether it was operating to socially responsible standards? That is not a flippant question for a large global business with a number of subsidiaries, with contractual arrangements to buy from a range of suppliers and to supply components to customers worldwide, and with a workforce of thousands spread across many sites in several countries. Even for a relatively small business, it can be difficult to keep track of the activities of all suppliers (especially when components are bought through an agent or wholesaler) or to know the ultimate use for all items sold as components to other companies who, in turn, manufacture further sub-assemblies to sell on. BT fell foul of this problem when it took over a business whose interests included premium lines, one of which offered a 'colourful' chat line service. Pornography is one of the absolute avoidance areas for ethical investors and so the situation briefly threatened BT's standing as a clean business. However, it was accepted that the

How would a business know whether it was operating to socially responsible standards?

company had not been aware of the nature of all interests held by the acquired business. BT has now instigated steps to avoid such an unplanned situation from arising in the future. For most investors or fund managers with a socially responsible agenda, it is the attitude reflected in how the company deals with the problem that says as much as anything about its general approach. Marks & Spencer similarly had to take Granada television to court over an implication that the store group had knowingly sourced products from a company that employed child labour. M&S won the case, not because there were no child workers involved in the production of their goods but because they were able to establish that the fact was not known to them. It pointed up the difficulties encountered by even the most scrupulous and thorough businesses in establishing a full awareness of all conditions throughout the operations of all suppliers worldwide.

Subsequently, M&S were the subject of a major study by EIRIS for the Ecumenical Council for Corporate Responsibility (ECCR) as a way of fine-tuning that body's set of benchmarks against which ethical standards may be measured. Although the store chain co-operated with the study, it was unable to provide full answers as to how it monitors any use of child labour by suppliers. Now, not many companies could provide that information and so the study should not be read as critical of M&S, rather their co-operation with the work should indicate the company's underlying morality, but it does point to the problems that may arise if a company, even when it has nothing to hide, cannot demonstrate that fact. In May 1998 when the findings of th study were delivered, EIRIS research head Stephen Hine commented: 'Companies increasingly have to recognize the need to publish details of this sort to maintain public confidence in their ethical claims. Nobody is saying that M&S doesn't care about child labour, but they weren't willing to give us details of their monitoring systems.'

Monitoring activities and identifying key information on ethical and environmental matters is an issue which might seem to require a whole new set of operating tools for business which, if it were the case, would probably mean a great deal of expense. But there is already a well established business practice which has provided the structure for a solution to this problem. When companies wish to know the full details of their financial and operational situation, they have an independent financial audit conducted by qualified accountants; indeed, an audit is the only way to unearth and be confident of the information that a business is required to include in the annual report and it is an annual event. Financial and operational audit trails throughout the business trace and value every component and operation, confirm its place in the process of the business and record

When businesses wish to know the full details of their ethical, corporate governance and environmental situation, they should conduct another audit.

a clear understanding of its contribution to the bottom line. So it is logical that, when businesses wish to know the full details of their ethical, corporate governance and environmental situation, they should conduct another audit. Social auditing is the process by which companies can establish the ethical and environmental credentials of the enterprise, monitor activities against their own declared standards of decent behaviour and find the information needed to improve their social, ethical and environmental performance. You may come across other terms in this context: terms such as environmental impact, ethical and social accounting, social balances and intellectual capital. They all refer to the same principle.

In a similar vein, which supports the view that ethical concerns are now moving centre stage in business, the Institute of Chartered Accountants in England and Wales (ICAEW) called on companies in June 1998 to review their corporate governance guidelines thoroughly in the light of the requirement of the new Combined Code on corporate governance published by the Stock Exchange. This is the first structural change to the shape of annual reports for a number of years and provides companies with an opportunity to take stock and to check that their governance disclosures are cohesive, concise and informative. Sir Brian Jenkins, Chairman of the Institute's Corporate Governance Group, commented: 'In their reports on governance, companies should focus on the measures that they have taken to ensure that the right board is in place and that it is working effectively.'

Ethical concerns are now moving centre stage in business.

These days, companies ignore the ethical and environmental dimensions of their operations at their peril. Size is no defence; indeed, the public often positively relishes the spectacle of a giant brought down. Corporate power cannot easily be deployed to limit the damage caused by revelations (whether proven or not, whether fair or not) of ethical or environmental shortcomings. McDonald's discovered that much when two campaigners distributed leaflets impugning the quality of the company's products. When the corporate giant won a lengthy court case, the financial cost had been enormous but that was not the worst cost the business incurred. The damage done to McDonald's image by two campaigners (apparently acting in accordance with honestly held principles and representing themselves in court) being crushed, albeit legally, by a global business was even more costly. The only way that a company can securely avoid such a situation arising in the first place is to establish its integrity beyond question through an independent report which addresses head-on any concerns that are voiced about the way it conducts its business, the manner in which it treats employees, the sources from which it buys in materials and components or the integrity with which it sells its products and services.

While a few years ago it might have been regarded as unnecessary for a company to justify its ethical, environmental and social performance alongside that of its financial results, the world has changed and some very big players have had to respond. Businesses do not come much larger, better established or respected than Shell. But the oil group found itself in environmental hot water over the way that it planned to dispose of life-expired rigs (the Brent Spar was the rig that brought this issue to the boil) and the perception that it made no effort at 'tidying up' behind its operations in third world countries. From this, people drew the inference, fair or not, that the business did not consider those countries to matter. At the same time, there were ethical difficulties over its apparent indifference to the human rights of people in countries, such as Nigeria, where it does business. Shell defeated a shareholders' motion calling for audited social reports at the 1997 Annual General Meeting but has since gone on to publish a new statement of business principles committing the group to act 'with honesty and integrity and respect for people.' Fine words but how would one know whether or not they had translated into operation policy? To meet this requirement, Shell has commissioned a social responsibility report and an audited environmental statement, both of which were published in 1998. There will also be a separate health, safety and environment report on all the group's activities and all its operating companies. The report, to be produced by the group's financial auditors, KPMG and Price Waterhouse, will include verification of management statements down to the lowest levels. If any evidence were necessary to show that the mightiest companies are coming to realize that the ethical and environmental agenda is not one to be ignored, this would be it.

Already in the USA, ethical fund managers take a pro-active stance, investing in businesses whose policies they wish to change.

Indeed, already in the USA, ethical fund managers take a pro-active stance, investing in businesses whose policies they wish to change and that investment approach is likely to reach these shores soon. It is the view of many leading lights of the ethical investment movement that such a policy would not only have a wider appeal but would also greatly increase both the profile of ethical funds and the notice which company boards took of them.

Generally agreed social and ethical accountability

When a business publishes its financial accounts, performance measurements are taken at pre-ordained points in the operation which are the same for all businesses and will be presented in an agreed manner to which all accountants have to work. That way, any observer and shareholder can compare the financial performances of different businesses knowing that they are comparing like with like. The problem with ethical or environmental standards and social responsibility is that, rather like ethics themselves, there could easily be as many standards as there are people and organizations practising them. An essential pre-requisite for proper auditing is the establishment of generally agreed standards of social and ethical conduct and accountability which carry the same clout as the generally agreed accounting principles do for the financial aspects of an operation. Then, businesses who submit themselves to a social audit under the agreed rules know that they will be subjected to the same scrutiny as others. The outcome of the audit will be respected and will honestly tell them and potential investors how they are doing against generally recognized standards of social responsibility, against their own objectives and compared to the performance of other businesses. It will also provide a framework within which to set their own objectives and the information from which a socially accountable corporate policy may be formulated, implemented and maintained.

The New Economics Foundation, which promotes the inclusion of ethical standards in business and sustainable development, set up the Institute of Social and Ethical Accountability (ISEA) in 1996 for the purpose of clarifying and agreeing standards against which social audits could be judged. Those standards having now been established, the ISEA offers training courses for those whose task it will be to produce social audits. It is this structured and organized approach to social accountability in business, placing it alongside financial accountability, that will get things done. A recent issue of the ISEA journal, 'AccountAbility' reiterated, in this context, a point that has always been true for any management strategy: what gets measured gets managed. Having agreed standards of measurement in a particular part of the operation removes any opportunities to hide behind phrases such as, 'It depends what you mean by . . . how you measure . . . ' and other evasive terms with which we have become wearily familiar over the years. It also makes much easier the task of focusing on improvement and of reporting the degree of improvement achieved.

Social accountability in the real world

In this chapter, much of the coverage is of principles, promises and the avoidance of punishments. If you are planning to invest some of your savings in a pension fund or other group investment fund which includes social accountability in its criteria of what is a good investment or if you plan to invest directly into shares of companies whose ethical and environmental qualities can be verified, that may not be enough to convince you that socially responsible practices have yet reached the real world. So let us take a closer look at three examples of the right way to do things. What they offer is examples of how social accountability in ethical and environmental matters can become part of the operation of three very different organizations. The first two cases, The Body Shop and British Telecom, are well known corporate names, although quite different businesses. The third case, The Centre for Tomorrow's Company, is not so much a business as a model established by the Royal Society of Arts to aid the evaluation of various ideas which aim to assist businesses and other organizations in developing better ways of working in a corporate environment, paying heed to ethical and environmental concerns as well as making a profit today and building the business for tomorrow.

A body of clear principles

There can be few businesses that have been more clearly identified by their efforts to work in a manner that supports sustainability and

balance than The Body Shop. As the fourth most selected stock for ethical fund managers in the 'Financial Director' survey (*see* Figure 8.1)
the business also meets the requirement that it provides a sound investment choice. More importantly, as The Body Shop ethical audit team
leader Maria Sillanpää explained, 'The ethical agenda in The Body
Shop is part of the company's mission statement,' which opens the
1997 Values Report, 'and is institutional-
ized into the DNA of the business.' The
whole ethical concept was driven by the
personal beliefs of the founders, Anita
and Gordon Roddick, children of the sixties who realized that protest is not
enough and that one has to do something

> *There is no point in a
> company being green if
> that means going out of
> business or being a drain
> on shareholders'
> resources.*

to make a difference. Funnily enough, some of the environmental
hallmarks of The Body Shop came about by accident, including the
recycling and refilling of bottles. That happened when the first shop
ran out of bottles at a time when the new stock would be a while in
delivery. Undaunted, the Roddicks asked customers to bring back their
used bottles for washing and refilling and so started what has become
a hallmark of the business. The overall plan has been to be entrepre-
neurial while, at the same time, saving resources.

The guiding social principles and policies of The Body Shop are
expressed in two key documents (Figures 8.1 and 8.2) – the mission
statement and the trading charter (both reproduced as examples of
how it can be done). These define social policies for which the business
is prepared to be accountable. Of equal note is the unashamedly commercial drive of the business; there is no point in a company being
green if that means going out of business or being a drain on shareholders' resources. Poor or weak management and business skills are
definitely not ethical and a failing business will add nothing of value to
society. It was with the introduction of both documents in 1994 that
striving for sustainability became enshrined in The Body Shop.
Sustainability is seen as part of an integrated approach to the business
which applies not only to materials but also to people and animals.
Overall, there are three bottom lines in this way of working; one for
profit, one for people and one for the environment.

Figure 8.1
THE BODY SHOP MISSION STATEMENT

- To dedicate our business to the pursuit of social and environmental change.

- To creatively balance the financial and human needs of our stakeholders: employees, customers, franchisees, suppliers and shareholders.

- To courageously ensure that our business is ecologically sustainable: meeting the needs of the present without compromising the future.

- To meaningfully contribute to local, national and international communities in which we trade, by adopting a code of conduct which ensures care, honesty, fairness and respect.

- To passionately campaign for the protection of the environment, human and civil rights and against animal testing within the cosmetics and toiletries industry.

- To tirelessly work to narrow the gap between principle and practice, whilst making fun, passion and care part of our daily lives.

The company's most recent social policy is a commitment to energy self-sufficiency. The Body Shop has invested (through a 15 per cent interest) in a Welsh wind farm. Fifteen per cent of the farm's output equals 25 per cent of The Body Shop's energy use and the plan is that eventually, this investment in sustainable energy generation will balance all of the firm's energy use.

Social audits have been part of the business since 1992 when the first external environmental audit was conducted and reported. Others have been added since then, including social and animal protection audits in 1996. The 1998 social audit was the first fully integrated exercise.

Maria Sillanpää believes that the whole process is a cycle of continuous improvement. Internally, that means agreed targets based on audit results and continuous improvement towards those targets as an objective. Externally, it means accountability and transparency

Figure 8.2

BODY SHOP TRADING CHARTER

The way we trade creates profits with principles

- We aim to achieve commercial success by meeting our customers' needs through the provision of high quality, good value products with exceptional service and relevant information which enables customers to make informed and responsible choices.

- Our trading relationships of every kind – with customers, franchisees and suppliers – will be commercially viable, mutually beneficial and based on trust and respect.

- Our trading principles reflect our core values.

- We aim to ensure that human and civil rights, as set out in the Universal Declaration of Human Rights, are respected throughout our business activities. We will establish a framework based on this declaration to include criteria for workers' rights embracing a safe, healthy working environment, fair wages, no discrimination on the basis of race, creed, gender or sexual orientation or physical coercion of any kind.

- We will support long term, sustainable relationships with communities in need. We will pay special attention to those minority groups, women and disadvantaged peoples who are socially and economically marginalized.

- We will use environmentally sustainable resources wherever technically and economically viable. Our purchasing will be based on a system of screening and investigation of the ecological credentials of our finished products, ingredients, packaging and suppliers.

- We will promote animal protection throughout our business activities. We are against animal testing in the cosmetics and toiletries industry. We will not test ingredients or products on animals, nor will we commission others to do so on our behalf. We will use our purchasing power to stop suppliers' animal testing.

- We will institute appropriate monitoring, auditing and disclosure mechanisms to ensure our accountability and demonstrate our compliance with these principles.

towards all stakeholders with whom the business is associated. That includes shareholders, employees, suppliers and customers. And there were one or two surprises from the first audits, even for a company so closely associated with social policies as this.

The first social audit confirmed a high quality, positive perception of The Body Shop among the various stakeholder groups but the first supplier survey held a surprise. In response to the question, 'I have never encountered any unethical behaviour in dealings with members of The Body Shop staff.' Eight per cent disagreed, while a similar number disagreed with the statement, 'We have never experienced any ethically corrupt behaviour in our dealings with individual members of The Body Shop staff.' While eight per cent is a low figure, it was unacceptable for a business built on the perception of fair dealing. New conduct targets were set and enshrined in a code of conduct for buyers to ensure propriety at all times. In this way, the process had identified and measured a problem and led to a structured and measurable response. It can be done and it can be done in a way which conforms with the normal planning and monitoring process that a company establishes for its performance in all other areas. It is also the information which such an approach will generate that will enable the managers of socially responsible funds to evaluate and select their stocks.

Communicating the right message

British Telecom (BT) is not the type of business that newcomers to socially accountable investment might first think of. It is one of the largest and most profitable companies in the world and there is a commonly held misconception that large, profitable companies have to be voracious in their dealings as well as unscrupulous in their treatment of people. Wrong; BT is the stock which appeared in more funds than any other in the *Financial Director* survey (*see* Table 8.1). That is good because, if ethical, environmental or socially accountable investment is to have any impact, it cannot be restricted to small businesses knitting things and bottling herbal potions and must be profitable to the investor. BT is in fact an excellent example of the values that ethical and environmental investors hold dear. It provides communication which uses a minimum of energy and can replace a number of energy-hungry alternatives. From the high technology of videoconferencing which might save several air journeys or journeys by rail and road, to the now routine system of electronic mail which can send very large documents across the country or the world in minutes and at far less cost in time or money than the equivalent delivery by ordinary mail might take. It is a business that has consistently reduced its prices and improved its service over the years since it became a privatized corporation and now actively looks to its own ethical and environmental performance.

BT's environment manager tells us that the company's policy covers two aspects of social accountability. 'We want to be a responsible company that minimizes its impact on people and the environment and we are in a unique position with a business whose products actually help to reduce

What is good for our business is usually also good for the environment.

the impact of other people, businesses and their activities. So, what is good for our business is usually also good for the environment.'

One key policy is the regular monitoring of energy used by the telephone system. Although the system uses less power than any form of transport, except walking and cycling (which may not be much use to people who are countries apart), it does, nonetheless, use energy. The amount of energy consumed does not vary much between when the system is idle and when it is in use but it is important to know what the energy requirement is for an average distance call for an average time in order to establish a target against which efficiencies can be measured. Where there are variations in energy consumption, they are often in the cost of running the hardware in the exchange. For instance, some of the energy consumption is to keep the equipment cool and one programme saw BT approach equipment manufacturers to see whether exchanges could be built to higher temperature tolerances. This has been achieved and new telephone exchanges now being installed use less energy because they can be cooled with fans alone rather than needing energy-hungry air conditioning. A spin-off benefit is that no CFCs are used in new exchanges – less energy consumption and less potential for pollution. Although most BT products are environmentally responsible, the least known one which has the most potential to save travel costs and time is audioconferencing. Cheaper than videoconferencing, audio-conferencing can be used by any group of people who are geographically dispersed but whose work would benefit from regular meetings.

One policy about which the public would know very little is the staff relations programme. BT encourages suggestions and involvement on the grounds that people are a long time at work and so should feel part of it and be proud of 'their' business. Staff are a very important stake-holder group, in many ways pivotal to the business's relationships with the world at large. Well treated staff whose opinions are valued are more likely, by disposition, to act well towards other stakeholders and to support the objectives of shareholders.

One of the things that have been learnt from the audits is that, when equipment fails (from a satellite receiving dish to a public call box), the sooner it is fixed, the lower the cost. So, what might be regarded as an environmental and quality of service matter for much of BT's equip-ment is in fact, a matter of bottom-line cost effectiveness. And is it all worthwhile in pure commercial terms? Kelvin Currie, speaking for the company, confirms that it is very worthwhile. Not only does it save energy but it also adds value to the company's reputation; readers who have had any involvement with the colourful art of PR will know how much a company's reputation is worth. Telecommunications is a tough business with ever tighter margins where every plus point helps; whether that is the good opinion of customers, the loyalty of a well treated employee, a reputation for doing the right thing or the more traditional achievement of cost-effective operations. There could be no better indication that a socially responsible approach is good for busi-ness that the fact that BT has adopted such an approach.

Tomorrow's Company

This initiative from the RSA – The Centre for Tomorrow's Company – is not a company in the same sense that The Body Shop and BT are but is rather a consultancy and a test bed where new ideas can be devel-oped before they are let loose on companies who need to make profits.

Mark Goyder, the first head of the Centre for Tomorrow's Company, feels that the inclusive, stakeholder approach to business is an idea whose time has come. One objective of Tomorrow's Company is to establish good socially responsible practices in each business that uses its services, as part of that company's credo rather than as just another policy. He cites the car maker BMW. 'BMW has not simply built a reputation; it operates using a highly developed set of behaviours which are all based on the understanding that it is a high-tech business.' This extends not just to the cars but even to the service bays of dealers, which are usually glass walled to be wholly visible from the service reception, and to the clean cups in which customers are served coffee while waiting for their car to be returned. It is that attention to detail and unwavering commitment to the credo of social responsibility at every stage of the business which Tomorrow's Company seeks to instil in businesses using its consultancy services.

So, what impact?

There is no doubt that the success of companies like The Body Shop and BT, as well as the new approach to its wider responsibilities of a business such as Shell, reflect a growing awareness in the world of commerce that a policy which puts sustainable development, decent dealings and clean activities at the forefront of its mission will be a policy for long-term success. Among the pressures that have brought about this situation is the pressure of shareholders standing up at annual meetings and pointing out the financial risks and long-term costs of particular policies. Only the best informed shareholders can do this effectively and they tend to be the managers of the large group investment funds who have access to the research resources which can put a value on corporate activity using generally agreed standards. The more people that invest their own savings and capital through funds whose investment criteria single out companies which follow these policies, the more the policies and, more importantly, the good that they can do, will take root in business culture.

A small but noteworthy moral tale of these times appeared in *The Ethical Investor* (the newsletter of EIRIS) September/October 1998 issue.

Huntingdon challenged

Dramatic evidence of the effect ethical concerns can have on a company's share price was reported in *The Daily Telegraph* after a sudden fall in the price of the shares of Huntingdon Life Sciences occurred in June.

Shares in the pharmaceutical company dropped sharply amid rumours that someone was trying to offload 15 per cent of their stock. The company announced they knew of no reason for the fall, but countered that later by explaining the big institutional shareholder, Robert Fleming, had sold its whole 14.6 per cent stake.

Robert Fleming has not revealed the reason for the sale but *The Daily Telegraph* reported it was widely believed to be a result of a campaign to get institutions to sell shares in any companies involved in animal testing. The British Union for the Abolition of Vivisection (BUAV) is trying to persuade other shareholders to sell.

Huntingdon shares had already fallen substantially after a Channel 4 film, shot undercover in their laboratories, showed dogs being punched and shaken. The Home Office investigated the company and the firm had to suspend shares for three months from July 1997. A separate attempt to film the company's laboratories in New Jersey has been stopped by court action.

'It comes as no surprise that investors such as Robert Fleming Holdings and leading pharmaceutical companies have continued to shun Huntingdon Life Sciences,' said BUAV spokesperson Yvonne Taylor. 'BUAV believes that this controversial company should never have been reissued with its [animal testing] licence in the UK.'

'Green' investment has certainly had its impact in this case and, given the levels of public concern that such issues attract nowadays, what

> *'Green' investment has certainly had its impact.*

sensible management team would wish to jeopardize the value of its brand and hence the desirability and value of its shares by ignoring socially accountable elements in its business mix?

The impact of green investment will be enormous and the strength of that impact will bear a direct relationship to the numbers of ordinary investors who express their views in this most effective of languages, the language of money.

Chapter 9

PERFORMANCE: CAN YOU AFFORD TO PUT YOUR MONEY WHERE YOUR HEART IS?

The big one

What we are considering is an investment of hard earned money, your hard earned money: savings and capital set aside to provide for the future realization of a long cherished ambition; perhaps to put children or grandchildren through university, maybe to pay for a wedding, possibly a world cruise and visit with family in Australia, eventually to provide for retirement with dignity and in comfort without the need to compromise on quality of life including, if necessary, long-term care or, possibly, simply to provide a nest egg, the 'rainy day' fund that growing numbers of people realize will be needed for a future when the state cannot or will not provide. Therefore, all that has been covered in previous chapters will be no more than fine words unless a socially responsible investment delivers consistent high per-

No matter how concerned you may be to do the right thing, you will probably not wish to do it at any cost.

formance in a very competitive market for your money to be invested in collective funds. Given that your interest in combining decency with the need to get a good return is more than a passing whim, no matter how concerned you may be to do the right thing, you will probably not wish to do it at any cost. Nor should you. After all, if dumping bottles or paper in the appropriate collection bank incurred a financial penalty, would so many people be prepared to support those recycling programmes? If our attitude to organic as opposed to chemically grown food is any guide, given the chemical option or the organic alternative but at a higher price, all but the most committed consumers will opt for the lower price. People are happy to be socially responsible as long as the cost is not unreasonable. Equally, if socially responsible investment is to succeed, it has to attract substantial support. For the majority of savers and investors, especially those whose future well-being depends on the returns from their investment, underperformance cannot be acceptable. Also, the most compelling logic behind including ethical and ecological concerns in any process is that it will then be going with rather than against the natural order of things and so, in the longer term, it is the most efficient way to conduct business. More fine words! But will your investment suffer? Will there be an investment penalty as reward for a commitment to do the right thing? These are the big questions which must be answered.

No ethics in losses

It has been stated several times in this book that there are no ethics in losing money – not for the investor who needs performance and growth in order to meet investment objectives and certainly not for the

There are no ethics in losing money.

fund manager entrusted with the sound management of other people's money. If, in order to meet socially responsible principles, a company cannot make a profit, then it will soon be out of business and what value then could one put on a principled approach to work? Equally, if losses arise from a well meaning but poorly man-

There is no good reason why a decision to invest according to socially accountable criteria should also be a decision to sacrifice performance.

aged business, that can add no long-term value to its field of activity and weak management is itself unethical in most people's books. There is no good reason why a decision to invest according to socially accountable criteria should also be a decision to sacrifice performance

and the socially accountable, ethical or environmental investment movement would not get very far if that was the case. Indeed, it was this very concern – that ethical constraints would compromise a fund manager's ability to discharge his or her duty to do the best possible job for investors – that, in the UK at least, for so long delayed the approval necessary in order that 'green' funds could be authorized. Fortunately, the evidence suggests that it is not the case that ethics and performance are contradictory objectives.

That is not to say, though, that ethical and ecological funds always perform well any more than do funds operating to the more traditional investment criteria of growth and income opportunities. All sectors of all economies are subject to cyclical movements over varying terms. Equally, for there to be top performing stocks, there have to be badly performing stocks, and average performers. Again, this would be true of any group of stocks, however categorized. No investment can be immune from such cycles or such performance variations between different companies, but a good fund manager will be able to minimize the impact of any adverse trend and capitalize on the opportunity of any positive trend. Although not always recognized as occupying a sector in their own right (they are usually categorized under one of the equity fund groupings), socially accountable investment funds and their investments do share a number of characteristics that influence performance, but then that would also be true of any group of funds. Additionally, because the concept of an ethical business or investment is relatively new, comparisons do not go back very far and, in respect of the earlier days of the concept, do not really include enough funds to make a comparison.

However, an increasing body of data is being built up from which to draw conclusions about the performance, both relative to other investments and absolute.

Not better nor worse, but distinct

In the past, socially responsible funds have invested mainly in small companies for several reasons. During the early days of ethical business concerns, the ones which were most easily able to base their business practices on socially responsible

In the past, socially responsible funds have invested mainly in small companies.

principles were those which had no baggage of older practices and that, inevitably, meant new companies which were generally small. Larger businesses, rather like large ships, need some time if they are to change direction without creating too disruptive an impact on the operations and effectiveness of the enterprise. When any new idea comes along, large corporations, for all their hype, are unlikely to embrace it unless they can see immediate or very early profitability. For instance, the media world has embraced new technology ideas with all the enthusiasm that you would expect of a business whose value and profits are determined by the size of audience and who very quickly saw satellite, cable, digital and other developments as means to extend that audience and create a profit centre with each programme. On the other hand, ideas that may well better the lot of the human race and the environment but will not turn an immediate or fast profit or may even conflict with, rather than add value to, current products or services will be less enthusiastically embraced and it may sometimes require legislation to generate a wide adoption. Catalytic converters to reduce the quantity and toxicity of car emissions would be a good example of this latter type of development. Motor manufacturers at first 'pooh poohed' the idea and then claimed that the inclusion of converters would add too much to the cost of new cars. However, when it became obvious that there would be no choice (the US state of California made catalytic converters a requirement), the converters were built, the cost was minimal and companies began to advertize the converters as a plus point in their products.

Because of the diversity of their interests, some of the world's largest 'blue chip' companies have a vast matrix of relationships with subsidiaries, associate businesses, other members of an alliance, franchisees, license issuers, suppliers, customers and so on. For these reasons, it has historically been very difficult, with such complexity and in the absence of social auditing, to be sure of the ethical and ecological strengths and weaknesses of any large global business in its entirety. Socially responsible funds have often invested in small companies and been subject to the volatility of that sector in which companies, with little fat to hinder them when things go well or cushion them in harder times, often move between the extremes of performance. However, with companies such as British Telecom and Shell now committed to social as well as financial audits, as well as the likes of Boots and Kingfisher able to satisfy their criteria, it is becoming easier for socially accountable fund managers to invest in businesses traditionally regarded as 'blue chip'. Also, when in recent times, pharmaceuticals, alcohol, gambling and tobacco and bank shares led the market, socially responsible funds were largely unable to participate in those sectors or benefit from their market leading performance. If funds begin to take a proactive approach and invest in companies whose policy they would wish to influence, that will include a further number of large and successful businesses.

Some managers overcome the constraints of being bound to particular ethical or environmental criteria by offering a 'light green' investment approach which may take a pragmatic view of companies who have a planned programme of improvement but who have paced that programme so as not to cause any unscheduled calls on profits, such as for new, environmentally clean equipment to replace older and less environmentally friendly equipment before any replacement was planned. Equally, where an accelerated programme of equipment improvement might threaten jobs in the

> *Some managers overcome the constraints of being bound to particular ethical or environmental criteria by offering a 'light green' investment approach.*

short to medium term, as long as the improvement programme is in place and being implemented, the sustainable speed will usually be best. The combination of a proactive stance and light green credentials allows the fund manager greater freedom to select successful stock without the need to fly in the face of socially responsible criteria.

There are, of course, pros and cons to be weighed in any decision. The pros of socially accountable investment have already been addressed but investors should remember that the full return on ethically and ecologically sound business practices may take a while, just as the damage inflicted when companies ignored warnings about asbestos and other dangerous materials also took a while to materialize as costly legal proceedings (financially costly as well as in public relations terms). It is possible that if, for instance, you are within a short time of retirement, not all socially responsible investments will be suitable for the funds that you propose to use in retirement. It is for reasons such as this that the expertize of a financial adviser will be valuable.

The research service EIRIS explains the pros and cons as follows (*The Ethical Investor*, September/October 1998) :

> . . . the relative performance of companies chosen by ethical investors may be affected by a number of factors. These include:
>
> - effects on companies – ethical companies may compete by using, say, energy-saving technology or making changes ahead of legislation. But avoiding military contracts may well lose you profitable business.
> - effects on portfolios – ethical fund managers tend to know their narrower field better, but ethical portfolios may be adversely affected by less diversification and higher management costs. Ruling out certain sectors can affect performance if that sector happens to perform better or worse than the rest. And small companies can be volatile.
> - other effects – financial performance depends on the ethical criteria used – the more restrictive, the greater the possible positive or negative impact on performance – and on the fund manager, of course.
>
> Take advice on the financial implications of your approach.

The advice is no different to what one would suggest to any investor on choosing a particular investment sector, whether that was emerging markets, technology, socially responsible or any of the other sectors available.

New indices

In order to be able to make some valid performance comparisons between socially responsible and other similar investments, appropriate indices have been constructed by EIRIS and some fund management groups.

In 1998, EIRIS assembled five indices covering the period from 1991 to 1998. Each index represented a different approach to socially responsible investment and all but one performed broadly in line with the FTSE All-Share Index. The September/October 1998 issue of *The Ethical Investor* explained: 'The indexes build on research work by EIRIS and investment consulting firm BARRA in 1989, and also others. They show that fears about ethical investment . . . are unfounded.'

NPI launched the first socially responsible investment index in May 1998 and used the performances of 150 companies reckoned to have good track records on ethical and ecological matters. Included in the index are 37 of the largest companies from the FTSE 100 index, 36 medium-size companies taken from the FTSE 250 index and the rest are taken from the Small-Cap index of smaller businesses. This structure gives the index a fair spread which is comparable to the All-Share Index. The new index will provide a further means of comparing the performance of socially responsible sectors with other sectors in the years ahead and NPI calculate that their social index would have outperformed the FTSE All-Share Index over the eight years from when it was launched.

This book cannot offer advice to readers on the correct approach to match their own situations (once again, a financial adviser would be the best qualified for this task) but, as a generality, the evidence seems

Figure 9.1
HISTORICAL PERFORMANCE – CUMULATIVE TOTAL RETURN

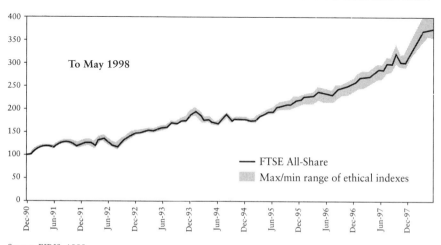

Source: EIRIS, 1998

to show that there has been no significant long-term performance disadvantage in investing in a socially responsible manner in the past and, fund for fund, if an investor had chosen the right one, he or she would have achieved an advantage. However, that statement would

There has been no significant long-term performance disadvantage in investing in a socially responsible manner.

be true of any investment. Equally, as the socially responsible sector matures, there is no reason to expect that its performance will vary wildly from the market as a whole. There are, though, sound reasons to expect that, in these

times where ethical and environmental issues occupy the top line on the agendas of most international bodies and the governments of the world's largest economies, socially responsible businesses will be at an advantage.

Comparative values

For our own purposes, we have put together a comparative table based on Standard & Poors Micropal Data about the UK market to give some idea of how various socially responsible funds have performed over a number of periods, both in absolute terms and relative to other funds in the same general sectors (*see* Table 9.1). All values are those achieved by 1 July 1998 for £1,000 invested one, two, three, five, seven and ten years earlier. The funds have been grouped according to their fund type – that is, unit trusts or Open-Ended Investment Companies (OEICs) (most unit trusts will convert to the more flexible and transparently priced OEICs before the end of the decade), insurance funds, investment trusts and pension funds. Within those groups, we have further grouped funds by the general sector which they occupy, rather than by specialist sectors – ethical or ecology. While the specialist sectors relate to the particular nature of socially responsible criteria which fund managers apply, the general sectors relate to the other investment criteria which are common to all funds whether or not they are socially responsible. Thus, an international equity growth fund will invest in the equity stock of businesses from around the world and which the fund manager

Table 9.1
CUMULATIVE PERFORMANCE STATISTICS OF
THE FIVE EIRIS INDEXES

Year end	Charities' avoidance	Environmental damage	Responders	Ethical balanced	Environmental management	FTSE All-Share
1991	26	28	23	17	25	21
1992	51	53	51	44	50	46
1993	88	94	91	91	83	87
1994	77	81	79	76	75	75
1995	117	124	122	114	109	118
1996	150	164	156	149	137	154
1997	218	232	232	213	204	214
1998	275	296	281	270	250	270

Source: The Ethical Investor, September/October, 1998

judges will see an appreciation in the underlying share value. The difference from other funds in that general sector will be that socially responsible fund managers will add to that set of criteria their ethical or ecological standards as appropriate. A UK equity income fund would, on the other hand, invest in the stock of UK companies which the fund manager judges will generate high levels of dividend and, thus, pay a good income in addition to the socially responsible criteria that these funds apply.

The columns are arranged in groups of three for each of the time periods over which performance has been measured. The first column for each period shows what value a £1,000 investment on the date in question at the head of the column would have achieved by 1 July 1998. The second column for each period shows the same performance but expressed as the percentage change in value between the date of investment and 1 July 1998. The third column in each group shows the fund's rank in its general sector. At the bottom of each fund type table, the best, average and worst results are shown and, last of all, the average or mean results for a comparable general sector.

Because there are several general sectors in each group, these cannot be read as direct comparisons. You would not normally, for instance, equate the performance of a growth fund with that of an income fund.

However, the purpose of the exercise is simply to help assess whether there is any significant advantage or disadvantage for investors who include ethical and ecological concerns in their investment criteria. In that context, it is the last four lines of each investment group that really count – the best, average and worst ethical funds and the average of the larger general sector which covers all of the general sectors listed. We have compared with average equity funds because all of the general sectors listed are either variants of equity funds or closely linked to performance in the equity sector. Nevertheless, this table is illustrative of a situation at a particular point in time; investors should always take advice regarding current data at the time of their investment and what might best suit their personal circumstances and preferred risk profile.

The Table

What is clear from Table 9.2 is that the findings of other indices – that there is no performance penalty for investing with a social agenda – are correct. There are a fair number of funds residing at or near the top of their general sector while others are well down. The reality is that, by the time you read this, some of the higher fliers will have fallen while some of the poorer results in this table will have been turned around into successes. What will not have changed is that there will continue to be a fair number at the top of their general sector as well as some who are well down the list. It is, though, very encouraging that, for most of the periods used in Table 9.2, the average socially responsible fund performed better than the average of the equity sector overall. What is clear is that, among ethical and ecological funds as among any group of funds, there are management teams whose past performance, while not an infallible guide to their future results, is better than others (which is true of any sector) and that investors with an agenda of social responsibility can demand performance for their investment just as any other investors would do.

Investors with an agenda of social responsibility can demand performance for their investment just as any other investors would do.

Table 9.2
COMPARATIVE PERFORMANCE

Value at 1 July 1998 of £1,000.00 invested on . . .

Funds	Specialist/General	Sector	01/07/97 Value	% Chg	Rank	01/07/96 Value	% Chg	Rank	03/07/95 Value	% Chg	Rank	01/07/93 Value	% Chg	Rank	01/07/91 Value	% Chg	Rank	01/07/88 Value	% Chg	Rank
UK Unit Trusts/OEICs																				
Equitable Ethical	Ethical	International Equity & Bond	1108	10.8	16	1183	18.3	12	1414	41.4	11	n/a	n/a	–	n/a	n/a	–	n/a	n/a	–
Henderson Ethical	Ethical	International Equity & Bond	1264	26.4	1	1332	33.2	5	1635	63.5	2	n/a	n/a	–	n/a	n/a	–	n/a	n/a	–
City Fincl Acorn Ethical	Ethical	International Equity Growth	1098	9.8	62	1142	14.2	95	1440	44.0	68	1581	58.1	78	2125	112.5	57	n/a	n/a	–
Clerical Med Evergreen	Ecology	International Equity Growth	1111	11.1	56	1113	11.3	103	1355	35.5	95	1286	28.6	110	1600	60.0	164	n/a	n/a	–
CIS Environ	Ecology	International Equity Growth	1249	24.9	7	1322	32.2	21	1582	58.2	26	1903	90.3	19	2680	168.0	15	n/a	n/a	–
AberdeenProl Ethical	Ethical	International Equity Growth	1097	9.7	63	1186	18.6	73	1465	46.5	58	1694	69.4	53	n/a	n/a	–	n/a	n/a	–
Jupiter Ecology	Ecology	International Equity Growth	1185	18.5	20	1258	25.8	43	1615	61.5	20	1899	89.9	20	2449	144.9	27	2940	194.0	29
Framlington Health	Ethical	International Equity Growth	979	-2.1	125	933	-6.7	131	1758	75.8	8	2221	122.1	9	3180	218.0	10	6617	561.7	3
NPI Global Care	Ecology	International Equity Growth	1217	21.7	12	1290	29.0	30	1604	60.4	23	1838	83.8	25	n/a	n/a	–	n/a	n/a	–
Friends Prov Stewardship Intl	Ethical	International Equity Growth	n/a	n/a	–	n/a	n/a	–	n/a	n/a	–	n/a	n/a	–	n/a	n/a	–	n/a	n/a	–
Allchurches Amity	Ethical	UK Equity Growth	1116	11.6	140	1266	26.6	123	1536	53.6	117	1659	65.9	116	2082	108.2	105	2695	169.5	65
Abbey Ethical	Ethical	UK Equity Growth	1196	19.6	95	1261	26.1	127	1565	56.5	113	1654	65.4	117	2265	126.5	99	2723	172.3	62
Credit Suisse Fellowship	Ethical	UK Equity Growth	1166	16.6	119	1191	19.1	137	1719	71.9	64	2233	123.3	16	2721	172.1	36	2437	143.7	80
Friends Prov Stewardship	Ethical	UK Equity Growth	1155	15.5	129	1240	24.0	131	1610	61.0	##	1840	84.0	98	2562	156.2	60	2622	162.2	69
TSB Environmental Investor	Ecology	UK Equity Growth	1287	28.7	15	1581	58.1	10	1931	93.1	13	2184	118.4	18	2825	182.5	30	n/a	n/a	–
Sovereign Ethical	Ethical	UK Equity Growth	1159	15.9	125	1156	15.6	143	1747	74.7	50	1913	91.3	82	2295	129.5	94	n/a	n/a	–
Scot Equitable Ethical	Ethical	UK Equity Growth	1160	16.0	123	1254	25.4	130	1670	67.0	79	1849	84.9	96	2401	140.1	80	n/a	n/a	–
Standard Lf UK Ethical	Ethical	UK Equity Growth	n/a	n/a	–	n/a	n/a	–	n/a	n/a	–	n/a	n/a	–	n/a	n/a	–	n/a	n/a	–
AXA Sun Life Ethical	Ethical	UK Equity Growth	n/a	n/a	–	n/a	n/a	–	n/a	n/a	–	n/a	n/a	–	n/a	n/a	–	n/a	n/a	–
Friends Prov Stewardship Inc	Ethical	UK Equity Income	1094	9.4	88	1057	5.7	87	1293	29.3	85	1505	50.5	76	2081	108.1	69	1987	98.7	67
NPI Global Care Income	Ethical	UK Equity Income	1262	26.2	12	1427	42.7	56	1870	87.0	3	n/a	n/a	–	n/a	n/a	–	n/a	n/a	–
Family Charities Ethical	Ethical	UK Growth & Income	1136	13.6	137	1244	24.4	129	1545	54.5	113	1898	89.8	81	2393	139.3	75	2921	192.1	51
FPAM Exempt Ethical	Ethical	UK Growth & Income	1287	28.7	9	1581	58.1	–	1931	93.1	–	2233	123.3	–	n/a	n/a	–	n/a	n/a	–
Best			1287	28.7		1581	58.1		1931	93.1		2233	123.3		3180	218.0		6617	561.7	
Average			1166	16.6		1233	23.3		1598	59.8		1822	82.2		2404	140.4		3118	211.8	
Worst			979	-2.1		933	-6.7		1293	29.3		1286	28.6		1600	60.0		1987	98.7	
UK UTs/OEICs Equity Funds (Mean)			1058	5.8		1191	19.1		1455	45.5		1763	76.3		2361	136.1		3036	203.6	

Table 9.2 cont.

Value at 1 July 1998 of £1,000.00 invested on . . .

Funds	Specialist	General	01/07/97 Value	01/07/97 % Chg	01/07/97 Rank	01/07/96 Value	01/07/96 % Chg	01/07/96 Rank	03/07/95 Value	03/07/95 % Chg	03/07/95 Rank	01/07/93 Value	01/07/93 % Chg	01/07/93 Rank	01/07/91 Value	01/07/91 % Chg	01/07/91 Rank	01/07/88 Value	01/07/88 % Chg	01/07/88 Rank
UK Insurance Funds																				
HFS Green Chip **	Ethical	Cautious Managed	1070	7.0	14	1081	8.1	28	1254	25.4	21	1402	40.2	12	1754	75.4	10	n/a	n/a	–
HFS Green Chip 2 – Exempt	Ethical	Friendly Society – Tax Exempt	1121	12.1	27	1115	11.5	40	1400	40.0	28	1643	64.3	23	n/a	n/a	–	n/a	n/a	–
HFS Green Chip – Exempt **	Ethical	Friendly Society – Tax Exempt	1104	10.4	31	1117	11.7	39	1360	36.0	30	1585	58.5	28	2061	106.1	21	n/a	n/a	–
Family Utd Chrties Ethical Ex	Ethical	Friendly Society – Tax Exempt	1158	15.8	15	1210	21.0	31	n/a	n/a	–	n/a	n/a	–	n/a	n/a	–	n/a	n/a	–
Clerical/Fidelity Evergreen	Ecology	International	1125	12.5	15	1114	11.4	67	1300	30.0	68	1263	26.3	133	1556	55.6	125	n/a	n/a	–
NPI Global Care	Ethical	International	n/a	n/a	–	n/a	n/a	–	n/a	n/a	–	n/a	n/a	–	n/a	n/a	–	n/a	n/a	–
Lincoln Green	Ethical	International	1116	11.6	21	1175	17.5	37	1435	43.5	21	1646	64.6	26	n/a	n/a	–	n/a	n/a	–
Equitable Lf Ethical	Ethical	International	1084	8.4	41	1151	15.1	49	1340	34.0	53	1487	48.7	184	n/a	n/a	–	n/a	n/a	–
HFS Green Chip 2	Ethical	Managed	1092	9.2	93	1084	8.4	231	1305	30.5	201	1691	69.1	26	n/a	n/a	–	n/a	n/a	–
Skandia Ethical Managed	Ethical	Managed	1127	12.7	30	1168	16.8	78	1475	47.5	22	n/a	n/a	–	n/a	n/a	–	n/a	n/a	–
NPI Global Care Managed	Ethical	Managed	n/a	n/a	–	n/a	n/a	–	n/a	n/a	–	n/a	n/a	–	n/a	n/a	–	n/a	n/a	–
Abbey Life Ethical	Ethical	UK Equity General	1160	16.0	122	1233	23.3	202	1464	46.4	177	1567	56.7	200	2040	104.0	151	n/a	n/a	–
Friends Provdnt Stewardship	Ethical	UK Equity General	1107	10.7	206	1192	19.2	208	1476	47.6	172	1662	66.2	175	2287	128.7	78	n/a	n/a	–
Eagle Star Environ Opps 1 **	Ecology	UK Equity General	1275	27.5	10	1413	41.3	37	1588	58.8	81	1921	92.1	37	2568	156.8	17	2364	136.4	124
Eagle Star Environ Opps 2	Ecology	UK Equity General	1294	29.4	3	1458	45.8	14	n/a	n/a	–	n/a	n/a	–	n/a	n/a	–	n/a	n/a	–
Scot Equitable Ethical	Ethical	UK Equity General	1137	13.7	204	1220	22.0	133	1543	54.3	164	1693	69.3	123	2151	115.1	124	n/a	n/a	–
FP Conscience (ex NM) **	Ethical	UK Equity General	1136	13.6	176	1175	17.5	210	1444	44.4	186	1638	63.8	182	2036	103.6	152	2331	133.1	125
Best			1294	29.4		1458	45.8		1588	58.8		1921	92.1		2568	156.8		2364	136.4	
Average			1140	14.0		1194	19.4		1414	41.4		1600	60.0		2057	105.7		2347	134.7	
Worst			1070	7.0		1081	8.1		1254	25.4		1263	26.3		1556	55.6		2331	133.1	
UK Life Funds Equity Funds (Mean)			1030	3.0		1129	12.9		1334	33.4		1556	55.6		1964	96.4		2509	150.9	
UK Investment Trusts																				
CU Environmental	Ethical	International Capital Growth	1218	21.8	9	1229	22.9	11	1552	55.2	8	1437	43.7	12	n/a	n/a	–	n/a	n/a	–
Jupiter Intl Green Units	Ecology	International Capital Growth	1199	19.9	10	1388	38.8	7	1537	53.7	10	1935	93.5	8	n/a	n/a	–	n/a	n/a	–
CU Environmental Wts	Ethical	Warrants	1357	35.7	54	1226	22.6	51	1583	58.3	36	1226	22.6	22	n/a	n/a	–	n/a	n/a	–
Jupiter Intl Green Wts	Ecology	Warrants	1625	62.5	35	1857	85.7	33	1733	73.3	29	2889	188.9	10	2737	173.7	6	n/a	n/a	–
Friends Prov Ethical Units (20)	Ethical	UK General	1101	10.1	19	1232	23.2	16	1428	42.8	14	n/a	n/a	–	n/a	n/a	–	n/a	n/a	–
Friends Prov Ethical–Ord (2001)	Ethical	(SC) Inc & Residual Cap Shs	1324	32.4	22	1334	33.4	21	1461	46.1	20	n/a	n/a	–	n/a	n/a	–	n/a	n/a	–
Jupiter Intl Green–Ord (2001)	Ecology	(SC) Inc & Residual Cap Shs	1473	47.3	16	1977	97.7	12	1859	85.9	14	2704	170.4	3	n/a	n/a	–	n/a	n/a	–

Table 9.2 cont.

			V	%	R	V	%	R	V	%	R	V	%	R	V	%	R	V	%	R
Friends Prov Ethic–Zero (2001)	(SC) Zero Dividend Pref Shs	Ethical	1074	7.4	19	1228	22.8	9	1456	45.4	6	n/a	n/a	–	n/a	n/a	–	n/a	n/a	–
Jupiter Intl Green–Zero (2001)	(SC) Zero Dividend Pref Shs	Ecology	1070	7.0	26	1182	18.2	18	1386	38.6	16	1593	59.3	7	2737	173.7		n/a	n/a	–
Best			1625	62.5		1977	97.7		1859	85.9		2889	188.9		2737	173.7		n/a	n/a	
Average			1271	27.1		1406	40.6		1555	55.5		1964	96.4		2737	173.7		n/a	n/a	
Worst			1070	7.0		1182	18.2		1386	38.6		1226	22.6		2737	173.7		n/a	n/a	
UK ITs Equity Funds (Mean)			1197	19.7		1366	36.6		1508	50.8		1984	98.4		2604	160.4		3760	276.0	
UK Individual Pensions																				
Abbey Life Ethical	Ethical	UK Equity General	1204	20.4	117	1284	28.4	203	1605	60.5	169	1730	73.0	188	2434	143.4	140	3103	210.3	81
Eagle Star Environ Opps 1 **	Ecology	UK Equity General	1344	34.4	6	1527	52.7	25	1744	74.4	73	2156	115.6	35	2951	195.1	23	n/a	n/a	–
Eagle Star Environ Opps 2	Ecology	UK Equity General	1393	39.3	2	1601	60.1	4	n/a	n/a	–	n/a	n/a	–	n/a	n/a	–	n/a	n/a	–
FP Conscience (ex NM) **	Ethical	UK Equity General	1167	16.7	187	1249	24.9	210	1617	61.7	163	1891	89.1	164	2417	141.7	143	2904	190.4	113
Friends Provdnt Stewardship	Ethical	UK Equity General	1184	18.4	164	1270	27.0	206	1665	66.5	142	1936	93.6	141	2848	184.8	37	3449	244.9	51
Scot Equitable Ethical	Ethical	UK Equity General	1166	16.6	192	1275	27.5	205	1697	69.7	119	1877	87.7	171	2572	157.2	112	2645	164.5	125
Standard Life Ethical	Ethical	UK Equity General	n/a	n/a	–	n/a	n/a	–	n/a	n/a	–	n/a	n/a	–	n/a	n/a	–	n/a	n/a	–
Winterthur/C Suisse Fellowshp	Ethical	UK Equity General	1277	27.7	23	1266	26.6	208	1374	37.4	64	1355	35.5	131	n/a	n/a	–	n/a	n/a	–
Clerical Med Perf Evergreen	Ecology	International	1136	13.6	21	1134	13.4	67	1414	41.4	53	1829	82.9	16	1709	70.9	127	n/a	n/a	–
Equitable Lf Ethical	Ethical	International	1111	11.1	37	1182	18.2	54	1573	57.3	17	n/a	n/a	–	n/a	n/a	–	n/a	n/a	–
Lincoln Green	Ethical	International	1158	15.8	17	1230	23.0	30	1891	89.1	3	n/a	n/a	–	n/a	n/a	–	n/a	n/a	–
NPI Global Care	Ethical	International	1279	27.9	4	1459	45.9	5	n/a	n/a	–	2214	121.4	5	n/a	n/a	–	n/a	n/a	–
NPI New App Global Care	Ethical	International	n/a	n/a	–	n/a	n/a	–	1764	76.4	7	n/a	n/a	–	n/a	n/a	–	n/a	n/a	–
Skandia/Framlngtn Health	Ethical	International	985	-1.5	123	930	-7.0	153	n/a	n/a	–	n/a	n/a	–	n/a	n/a	–	n/a	n/a	–
NPI Global Care Managed	Ethical	Managed	1221	22.1	9	1367	36.7	17	n/a	n/a	–	1906	90.6	28	n/a	n/a	–	n/a	n/a	–
NPI New App Global Care Mgd	Ethical	Managed	n/a	n/a	–	n/a	n/a	–	1634	63.4	18	n/a	n/a	–	n/a	n/a	–	n/a	n/a	–
Professional Lf Ethical Mgd	Ethical	Managed	1222	22.2	8	n/a	n/a	–	n/a	n/a	–	n/a	n/a	–	n/a	n/a	–	n/a	n/a	–
Skandia Ethical Managed	Ethical	Managed	1212	21.2	17	1243	24.3	181	n/a	n/a	–	n/a	n/a	–	n/a	n/a	–	n/a	n/a	–
Best			1393	39.3		1601	60.1		1891	89.1		2214	121.4		2951	195.1		3449	244.9	
Average			1204	20.4		1287	28.7		1634	63.4		1877	87.7		2489	148.9		3025	202.5	
Worst			985	-1.5		930	-7.0		1374	37.4		1355	35.5		1709	70.9		2645	164.5	
UK IP Equity Funds (Mean)			1051	5.1		1179	17.9		1425	42.5		1727	72.7		2290	129.0		3005	200.5	

Source: Standard & Poors Micropal.

This has not always been the case. But today, socially responsible investment is coming of age and is able to offer levels of performance that will appeal beyond the committed followers of that agenda to a wider investing public. People who would like their money to say, more loudly than they otherwise could, that business must not be lazy but must work to achieve the growth and success that shareholders demand without resorting to unethical or environmentally unfriendly methods. In doing that, socially responsible policies may even attract investors who have no such concerns themselves but are just looking for a profit.

What lies ahead?

Socially responsible, ethical, ecological, green . . . whatever you choose to call them, investment funds which include in their criteria the requirement that companies in which they invest must operate decently are here to stay and they are available now at no additional cost. The companies should also return a profit sufficient to ensure they remain strong and with access to whatever capital requirements there may be in order to continue to grow and develop the business. From investing in smaller companies they have seen some of those companies grow and mature as businesses. At the same time, the larger companies whose stocks traditionally stabilize funds are experiencing a growing awareness of the need to operate to socially responsible standards. Yes, because it is the decent thing to do but also because it is likely to be the best way to make sustainable long-term profits in a world where public attitudes to corporate behaviour are increasingly reflected in legislation to prescribe the way businesses are run. Not only are the socially responsible funds growing rapidly and outpacing the collective investment sector generally, but also the number of charities, local authorities and pension funds embracing socially responsible investment criteria are adding weight to the sector and volume to any views expressed by the sector. This will, in turn encourage even more fund managers to take that path and will mean that a significant number of institutional investors working to that agenda will be vocally present at the AGMs of those companies whose well-being depends, at least in part, on the judgement of their performance represented by the share price. As the process progresses, so increasing numbers of boards of directors and their management teams will have to take notice of the views of investors who care for all-round and sustainable added value. From being the investment arm of a protest movement, social responsibility is about to move centre stage as a key investment criterion which may one day be no more worthy of comment than the criterion that fund managers should endeavour to achieve the best possible return and growth for their investors.

The best scenario for the future of socially responsible investment is that investors will feel that they will be able to get the best value from a socially responsible fund. More and more people do feel that to be the case as well as those who have always felt that the ethics and morals of the investment overrode even their need for profit. An increasing body of evidence supports the

Socially responsible investment is a legitimate and productive mainstream investment choice.

view that the long-term benefits of such an investment policy balance any short-term disadvantages and ensure that socially responsible investment is a legitimate and productive mainstream investment choice.

Chapter 10

GREEN LEGISLATIVE AND OTHER OUTSIDE INFLUENCES

A changing background

If you are considering selecting a group investment which includes among its stock selection criteria an ethical dimension as well as an expectation that the business will generate profits through true added value while pursuing long-term developments that are sustainable, you are most probably motivated by moral considerations. However, there are also some very practical reasons why it would be sensible for an investor to consider the socially responsible, ethical or environmental investment sector. Holdings in a group investment ought to be for the long term in which case, investors would wish to be assured that their investment stood a better than even chance of prospering, delivering growth and income, well into the future because plans have been laid and actions undertaken to secure that objective. We have already seen how the

The management teams of businesses run along ethical and environmentally sustainable lines are viewed favourably for their planning and long-term thinking.

management teams of businesses run along ethical and environmentally sustainable lines are viewed favourably for their planning and long-term thinking. But, however good a management team may be, there are other factors which can bear on a business's ability to achieve long-term success – factors which are usually outside the control of any individual company. It would, of course, be easy to talk here about the current of social sentiment, the tide of public opinion and other such lofty notions but such factors are often quoted when there is no hard evidence on which to rely. While we will talk about those influences later on, the main part of this chapter will be considering developments in the legislative climate whose effect would be to make life more difficult for businesses which disregard ethics, sustainability and their broader responsibilities to society.

The other side of this coin is that the same legislation will mean businesses who have set out their ethical and environmental agenda and have put into place the means to monitor and adhere to that agenda, will find themselves swimming with the tide of national and supranational policy, inasmuch as legislation in western economies reflects that policy. They will certainly find it easier to operate within a legal structure that formalizes particular positive attitudes and decent standards of corporate behaviour.

Given the nature of governments in the major economies of Europe and America today (their reliance on focus groups, the need to be re-elected, etc.), there is also a likelihood that, if enough people express a strong view in favour of a particular attitude or policy, the government will wish at least to appear to be moving in the same direction. So, a strong movement towards ethical and environmental dimensions in investment policy would encourage a government to consider how it might be seen to be going with that tide. This certainly appears to be happening in the United Kingdom where several government ministers have made pronouncements of positive attitudes regarding ethical and environmental issues. If and when they are translated into legislation and policy, these attitudes, will have a significant effect on the conduct of business in the areas affected. So it will be a good idea to examine what is happening in these areas now and what that might mean for the future. One note of caution, though.

The content of this chapter includes only an illustrative selection of initiatives and policies with ethical and environmental implications. I would strongly advise that socially responsible investors keep up to date with the latest developments in the thoughts and actions of government and supra-governmental organizations (such as United Nations agencies) for pointers to what the future holds, as any sensible investor would wish to do in order to avoid investing in businesses whose modus operandi may, in the foreseeable future, bring them into conflict with what is legally acceptable.

The whole area of policy and legislation has to be seen in the context of a growing awareness that the warnings and predictions of environmentalists as well as the expressed concerns of campaigners on ethical issues were not simply the rantings of committed activists. But that has been a problem and it must be said that the manner in which some campaigners have put their case has often overshadowed the case itself. Some ill-advised pronouncements have been made which have given fodder to parts of the press who wished to portray activists as barmy. During a protest against the transport of live veal calves from the UK to Europe, one well known personality was told by a lorry driver that he had to feed his family. Quite an understandable point of view, you might think. The personality retorted that the driver's family was of no interest and, in a few words, reinforced the notion that protesters can be out of touch with reality. This provided free copy for anybody who wished to argue against what was, generally, a sincerely held moral stance against a particularly unpleasant form of animal exploitation. Good cause, atrocious communication. Emotions around environmental and ethical issues of the day have often run high with the result that passion has eclipsed reason. However, most of the protests have been based on genuine concerns that emanate from sound research and recorded trends in the environment. With mainstream scientists now confirming that the environmental disasters first predicted by groups such as Greenpeace and Friends of the Earth (and largely rejected by the scientific and political establishments at that time) really are waiting just around the corner, most reasonable people and even governments have had to take note. With the powerful 'me first' sentiments of the 1980s now being replaced by the more '*communitaire*' approach of the 1990s, we are seeing the current socio-economic cycle enter its second phase and take a step nearer to maturity. That is if you believe that a society is a little like an enterprise which, traditionally, moves from a buccaneering to a reflective and then to a mature style.

On the ethical front, much the same would be true. Concerns on ethical issues have tended to be regarded as getting in the way of progress and the theory has been that, if the people at the top of the line prosper, prosperity will cascade down the line to increase the well-being of all, even if the differentials remained the same. However, in global terms and within any population group or work group, the reality has been that the rich, the aggressive and those with particular profit-focused skills have prospered mightily while those who were less fortunate have seen their relative (and sometimes their absolute) situation deteriorate. It does seem that some adjustments will need to be made to the way we behave in order for a balance of opportunity and progress between rich and poor to be restored.

On these, as on many other issues, governments have started to create policies taking account of the public's growing interest in thinking ahead, thinking sustainable, thinking honest and decent, and thinking fair. There are not many overtly ethical or environmental measures but there are many policy pointers that make it clear that those values will, in future, hold an important part in the thinking of governments around the world.

All around the world

A cynic might say that the further up the governmental and supra-governmental ladder you look, the more likely people are to have their heads in the clouds which would make most supra-governmental efforts for the environment and ethics pretty much a waste of time. There is also the less cynical approach which understands that, in order to get a pronouncement which is acceptable to a majority of the world's nations, it will not be possible to get much more controversial than stating that water is wet and air is dry. So, events such as the earth summits at Rio in 1992 and Kyoto in 1997 will necessarily have been long on 'motherhood and apple pie' but short on what to do about the environment or action plans to achieve even their limited objectives. However, we should not dismiss them for all that. Even if they make no immediate difference to the way the world works, the publicity generated and the issues aired help to set an agenda for national and local governments to make policy appropriate to their own requirements and priorities. And if that means compromises, well, so be it. Limited progress, hedged with caveats and generous timescales, is better than no movement at all and is more likely to be achievable. It also establishes a new and higher base line from which to set a future agenda for even more progress.

Also, such summits do often get governments to commit to standards that they might otherwise try to fudge. For instance, at Rio, the developed nations agreed to a set of, albeit voluntary, targets on emission levels. They agreed to take measures aimed at lowering emissions of carbon dioxide and other greenhouse gases to 1990 levels by the year 2000. A small step, but at the follow-up environmental conference held in Kyoto, the developed nations signed up to a 174 nation agreement (this time legally binding) to reduce emissions of those same gases, over the period 2008–2012, to 5.2 per cent below 1990 levels. Within those overall targets, the member states of the European Union agreed to undertake an 8 per cent re-

> *Summits do often get governments to commit to standards which they might otherwise try to fudge.*

duction in recognition of the high proportion of world-wide greenhouse gas emissions that occur in the EU. Furthermore, within even that challenging target, the UK has agreed to target a 12.5 per cent reduction. This will be difficult news for businesses engaged in processes which generate greenhouse gases and which have not, as yet, formulated or started to implement policies which will see them coping with the new limits as a normal part of a planned programme of improvement. They may have to start from scratch and divert productive resources to this essential but non-productive task.

However, it does bode well for the manufacturers of equipment to generate power from renewable resources such as wind power, wave power and even from burning wood as the latest power plants do (wood is a renewable resource if farmed just to provide fuel). It is also good news for companies whose management teams have had the foresight to plan a steady rate of improvement in the cleanliness and sustainability of their processes. This is all useful information for investors and not only those with a socially responsible agenda. No investor or investment manager would wish to be tied into a business which, at best, faces an uphill struggle and, at worst, will be vulnerable to all sorts of attacks while management efforts are focused on catching up with the real world rather than growing and developing the business. And when it has all been done, who is to say that markets lost, while management's eye is 'off the ball', will ever be regained?

One other area in which the international efforts have made a great deal of progress is in the eradication of disease. This is not a matter of legislation but the key organizations that do the work on the ground (inoculation campaigns, for example) get a great deal of moral and financial support from governments. As the spectre of disease recedes, so the economies of the countries in question can begin to focus on projects for economic progress. This may well benefit the type of businesses who promote fair trade and the types of enterprise who provide basic economic requirements such as water purification plant and agricultural equipment as well as the more sophisticated pharmaceutical, medical and surgical products that bring about the reduction and elimination of disease.

Brussels rules, OK!

There is, though, a level of supra-national government which not only has a consistent policy on ethical and environmental issues but also has increasing power to project that policy into legislation at a national government level. The European Union started out as a trading zone called the European Common Market with an internal tariff structure to encourage trade among the member states in a manner which would enable companies in those states to enjoy economies of scale that can only be achieved in a very large market. That, though, was a very long time ago and now, with a single currency and with a quite distinct social democrat slant on capitalism and economics, the European Union is well on the way to becoming a single economic and political entity which, whether you agree with that or not, will stamp a distinctive style on the legislative programmes of member states. Already, in areas such as working hours, works councils, annual leave, health and safety and a host of other areas, European legislation takes precedence over local law and European legislation has a high content of ethical considerations and environmental objectives. While the individual directives would be too numerous to specify, we are becoming familiar with the changes in our water purity regulations, the conservation of fish stocks, working time directives, the social chapter, human rights rulings from the European Court of Human Rights (not strictly an EU institution but who can tell the difference?), even the packaging of products on our supermarket shelves. One recent intervention from Europe was the ban on worldwide exports of British beef because of fears that the meat might be contaminated with the BSE virus which may be linked to the human condition Creutzfeld

European legislation takes precedence over local law and European legislation has a high content of ethical considerations and environmental objectives.

Jacob's Disease (CJD) and a new variant of that condition which appeared at about the same time that the BSE crisis was in full flow. Such ethical or environmental concern should sound a warning to businesses that poor behaviour in areas where the environment or the general well-being of people could be adversely affected will not be possible, at least not within the law.

This bodes well for businesses which have been cleaning their processes, trying to find better ways of disposing of waste or recycling it, removing unnecessary chemicals from the products they make and according their workforce the type of decent work conditions and consultation channels as stakeholders in the business that will add motivation and ensure that everybody, having participated in the decision process, understands the thinking behind policy and plans. Workers may also have an opportunity to suggest alternative ways forward that might well incorporate the direct experience from the sharp end that no business model can ever replicate. On the other hand, this bodes ill for businesses who have steadfastly ignored the opportunities to improve their processes and their work practices on the grounds of cost or because they do not trust their workforce. Such businesses will find it a struggle in the short term to match the latest standards, build goodwill in the business and continue to devote the resources that the business requires to operate profitably. Their exclusion from fund stock lists will not need to be on moral grounds but on the simple grounds that they have burdened themselves with an unnecessary additional and non-productive workload and have demonstrated a management style that does not suggest the business is good at looking ahead or managing change.

Nearer to home

When the present UK government came to power, they promised action on a number of fronts including various pledges that there would be a more human, more ethical approach to some key matters of policy. Now, whenever politicians speak of ethics (or anything, come to that) they will have in mind votes and what actions will please the most people while alienating the least number. Nevertheless, there have been a number of initiatives from the Labour government in the UK which, if translated into real actions, will see British policy at home and in the world at large taking into account the moral and environmental dimension to a greater extent than ever before.

There is an extent to which only a new government can do this as they have a large stock of public goodwill to absorb some of the less immediately popular decisions that must be made. People are very contradictory, especially when it comes to ethical and environmental issues. For instance, everybody would agree that there should be less use of cars and yet all would also find that their own use of a car is virtually indispensable. The public also have a healthy cynicism for any policy that involves a payment to a government body at national or local level. And, unless payments which are designed to discourage environmentally damaging behaviour (road pricing, etc.) can be clearly seen to be doing a job which will make the environmental alternative better, people will choose not to re-elect that government when the opportunity arises. It may be that they are voting against the unethical policy of charging for the behaviour to be discouraged rather than investing in the infrastructure to enable the behaviour to be encouraged.

Foreign affairs

On assuming the mantle of Foreign Secretary in 1997, Robin Cook declared that his would be an ethical foreign policy. The theory is that

UK policy overseas should put the pursuit of human rights matters before the need to secure orders for UK companies. Also, if the policy is to be ethical in a pure sense, it will avoid the sales of arms to regimes with poor records on human rights or coexistence with their neighbours. However, and this is the rub, if we do not sell those arms the immediate effect will be a loss of jobs in the UK at the factories which supplied those weapons and, probably, the creation of jobs in France or another arms-producing economy which will gladly take on the business. Therefore, it is a fine line that the government has to follow between a pure ethical policy and the well-being of workers (many of whom will have voted for them) at home. And how ethical is it to cut off somebody's livelihood without taking the trouble to find an alternative for them first? Nevertheless, in anticipation of the long term, a number of defence businesses are diversifying and, while that may not make them natural candidates for socially responsible fund managers, it will mean that the areas into which they move will become more competitive and their likely dominance of new sectors into which they enter may mean that the companies most likely to succeed are those who can offer the kind of personal, bespoke service which industrial giants sometimes find difficult. However, not far from the Foreign Affairs brief is the Overseas Development brief where the UK is implementing a different approach which seeks to help developing countries with what they need rather than what we have to sell. Although the present policy is not to tie aid to trade or other contracts, there must be a beneficial effect on businesses whose stock in trade includes the basic needs of developing economies. Water purification plant, simple transport systems, low-cost and easy-maintenance agricultural machinery, clockwork radios, disaster relief equipment, field medical units that can cope with the overwhelming majority of life threatening conditions and low-technology power generation all spring to mind. On the other hand, it may mean less work for the large building consortia who have provided the developed world with projects such as prestigious airports and buildings to compete for the title of world's tallest, largest, etc., whose relevance is at best dubious and at worst non-existent.

The road to clean air

There is little doubt that the motor car is one of those boons of the twentieth century that has made possible comfort and mobility on a scale unheard of in previous centuries to a class and number of people who might never have left their home village in past times. But it is a terrible boon nonetheless because it delivers its bounty at a very high price. From stress, to pollution and the despoliation of the countryside for roadbuilding, the downside of motoring has been well documented. So the current UK government has tried to formalize some targets on stabilization and reduction of pollution levels from cars as part of a broader policy direction with regard to pollution. In November 1998, the UK Climate Change Programme was launched with a consultation paper from the Department of the Environment, Transport and the Regions (DETR) and the equivalent authorities in Scotland, Wales and Northern Ireland. The foreword to that document concludes with the following words.

'This consultation paper is designed to stimulate a national debate on how we might meet our targets [for reductions in pollution levels]. We are one of the first countries to publish such detailed ideas since Kyoto. We are inviting views at this early stage to ensure that we have a good understanding of what can be achieved practically and cost effectively. We are determined to meet our targets in ways which enhance rather than damage UK competitiveness and which increase social inclusion. We also want to hear about any more imaginative and longer-term ideas. We know that we do not have all the answers. Solutions will require partnerships between Government, industry, voluntary groups and individuals.

After this consultation is complete, we will develop and consult further on a new climate change programme for the UK. Above all, we want to create real commitment across the UK to tackling climate change. Climate change is a threat to us all and to our children. But it is also an opportunity to change society for the better. We must now deliver on our promises.'

Fine words but how will they be translated into action? Voluntary arrangements may go some of the way and there will be some scope for the government reaching agreement with individual sectors without any need for recourse to legislation (the agreement to end animal testing of cosmetics would be an example to follow). However, the only way that the fine words above will become practice will be if the government legislates and we can discern the tone of future legislation on issues which affect ethics and the environment.

Can that be sustained?

The UK government has also declared its hand on the issue of sustainable business. In this policy, the link between prudent use of precious resources and the future sustainability of our lifestyle is clearly drawn in the opening words of the same consultation document from the DETR.

> 'The Government is committed to sustainable development, combining economic, environmental and social objectives [for performance in] . . . social progress . . . protection of the environment . . . prudent use of natural resources . . . maintenance of high and stable levels of growth and employment.
>
> These objectives are closely linked. For example, protecting the environment is not necessary just for its own sake but because a damaged environment will sooner or later hold back economic growth.'

The document goes on to look at the opportunities and challenges that the new policy on sustainable development will set for businesses. In a section entitled 'The Sustainability Challenge', the document sets out three levels of action which will be necessary in order for a sustainable development policy to work. Right at the top of that list is the statement:

> 'Government must set a long-term and consistent policy framework, putting in place the correct economic instruments, regulations and incentives for business and consumers.'

Clearly, the UK government intends that its drive for sustainable development will not simply be fine words but will also involve government action through the legislative programme. Further on the document asks:

'Where are the responsibilities for the issues raised by sustainable development held within your business?'

Many pointers to the future

A further pointer to the moral attitude of the present UK government can be seen in the enactment of regulations on late payments. Although phased over a number of years, these regulations, which will first apply to large organizations making payment to small businesses, will eventually make it very difficult to make late payments and will allow creditors to charge a statutory level of interest on late payments.

The UK government will be passing laws whose effect will be to disadvantage businesses whose drive for profits has ignored the moral or long-term sustainability dimension. At the same time, legislation is likely to favour businesses who have planned ahead, have already considered the ethical and environmental aspects of their work and have established a programme of business development to translate those considerations into reality. Even if you were unconvinced by the moral

It is becoming clear that not to act in a socially responsible manner is not going to be a viable option for UK businesses.

argument for socially responsible investment, it is becoming clear that not to act in a socially responsible manner is not going to be a viable option for UK businesses or for businesses dealing with the UK. This will also be true of the European Union, in which the UK is a major component. So, if a business wishes to have access to these large markets, it will need to be able to comply with whatever regulations concerning the ethical and ecological aspects of operation that may be applicable in the EU or UK. As an investor concerned just with the long-term prospects that an investment will perform, are you likely to put money into a business that faces some years of upheaval while the management team tries to keep up with the changes brought about by a legislative programme that favours work methods and operational standards that the business has previously ignored? Can you really have faith in the capability of managers to deal with a requirement to change in which they have previously shown no particular interest, skill or foresight? Or will investors favour those businesses which have already embraced the best practice in areas of ethical and ecological dimensions and who can face any ethical and environmental development of business law without equivocation, safe in the certainty that the business already operates in a manner that embraces the principles of decency and sustainability enshrined in new legislation?

The reality is that it is not simply a good or a decent thing for investors to include a moral and sustainability dimension into their investment criteria. To be working in a way that takes account of those issues is to be working in a way which will easily settle in to the new legislative climate promised by governments around the world – whether it be the reduction of pollution from cars or the provision of public transport; in the reduction or elimination of harmful emissions of greenhouse gases in processes of the business or the creation of non-degradable waste products; through the decent treatment of workers as human and valuable stakeholders in the business in fair return for the investment of their labour and skills; through honesty in dealings with other parties (suppliers and customers) and transparency in reporting on the activities of the business. In all of these areas, businesses can show themselves to be thinking ahead and in tune with the realization that profit at the expense of honesty, of the decent and fair treatment of others or of resources being used that cannot be replaced, is not so much profit as theft from other people today or from our children tomorrow.

At this stage, many of the ideas may seem to be remote or unworkable but if experience with the European Union has taught us anything, it is that, once a legislative course has been set, there is no stopping. The only limiting factor is how long it may take to implement. The current Labour government in the UK has learned from this and only a reckless business would now ignore the need for moral and ecological dimensions to business practice. Certainly, to invest in businesses of the type that socially responsible funds would choose is likely to look very sensible on economic and financial grounds as well as on grounds of conscience.

And there is plenty of evidence that even current legislation and regulation can allow for businesses who ignore the reality to suffer an appropriate financial penalty. Companies which fall foul of current health and safety regulations are frequently fined, with both the Health and Safety Executive and Trades Unions taking an active approach to ensuring that workers' welfare is not compromized for any reason. Equally, readers will be aware of the regular and well publicized prosecutions which follow major incidents of water pollution.

As further indicators of their intent regarding the ethical dimension in business, the Labour government in 1999 put into law a national minimum wage and introduced legislation to translate the Fairness at Work elements of the EU Social Chapter into UK law. Both of these measures will make it more difficult for employers to treat workers badly or to deny them their 'rights' in a number of key areas of employment practice. Although each legislative development on its own may not cause too much additional work for a business, taken together they add up to a legislative climate that positively favours companies whose operations are already ethical and inclusive for shareholders, management and workforce.

It is not only legislation that affects the climate within which businesses operate or their behaviour. Only a very reckless management team would ignore the positive and negative ebbs and flows of public opinion. Fickle it is, illogical it can be, more herd instinct than individually considered understanding it may be but, of course, no single member of the public would ever know that was how their opinions are formed. Many really do hold the views that they espouse, resulting from con-

> *Only a very reckless management team would ignore the positive and negative ebbs and flows of public opinion.*

sideration based on facts and, however it has been arrived at, an opinion is a very influential moderator for our view of the world, what is right and what is wrong. Increasingly today, public opinion, as reflected in (moulded by) the popular press, is moving away from the worship of the unfettered capitalism that typified the 1980s and towards what is perceived to be a more balanced view of wealth generation within a society which places equal value on all of its members, regardless of their wealth or ability. Socialism it is not and, while to go too far down this road is as dangerous as any extreme, most people feel instinctively more comfortable with a balanced society than one which takes an extreme approach. Equally, the protests of the eco-warriors and others whose efforts have brought to our attention issues which might otherwise have been buried and forgotten, while they may have attracted censure in themselves, have succeeded

Businesses must react to shifts in the public's attitudes.

in raising public awareness of those activities which are spoiling the world around us and reducing its capacity to support us and our children. Businesses must react to shifts in the public's attitudes because, no matter how they have been arrived at, the opinions of the public will influence the sales and financial success of a business. That is why some of the very largest corporations on earth are focusing so much effort on their ethical and environmental policies and why they are accommodating views that they might have rejected out of hand just a few years ago.

There are no laws as yet compelling the British Airways and British Telecoms of this world to take social and ecological issues into account or to instigate environmental audits of their business activities. But very large and successful businesses want to remain that way and will not undertake a policy which is likely to bring bad publicity or offend public opinion even if they could legally do so. Some might say that public opinion is the real law of the market rather like a law of nature. Certainly, public

Certainly, public opinion is now swinging towards favouring the types of businesses which can show a clean ethical and environmental bill of health.

opinion is now swinging towards favouring the types of businesses which can show a clean ethical and environmental bill of health and investment managers will not ignore such factors in their calculations.

Perhaps we can hope that, in the longer term, the need for a separate

Ethical investors have already established for themselves a place in the future.

ethical and environmental investment sector will disappear as practice, policy and track record in these areas begin to rank alongside the more traditional criteria for a good investment. However, until that time, the more discerning investors who do include criteria of conscience into their investment thinking will be comfortable in the knowledge that, as ethical investors, they have already established for themselves a place in the future.

Part 5

DIRECTORY OF FUNDS AND INDEPENDENT FINANCIAL ADVISERS

Chapter 11

THE WHO, WHY AND WHEREFORE OF ETHICAL INVESTMENT OPPORTUNITIES

A growing sector

As the ethical investment phenomenon has grown, so the range of funds available to investors concerned about the broader implications of human activities has also grown to meet demand. The first Stewardship Fund was launched by Friends Provident in 1984. By 1998, there were 23 UK Unit Trusts and Open-ended Investment Companies (OEICs), 17 UK Insurance Funds, 9 UK Investment Trusts and 18 UK Individual Pension Funds listed by Standard & Poor's Micropal (*see* Appendix) in the Ethical and Ecology Specialist Sectors. These 67 funds were managed by 27 fund management groups but the sector is still growing and there may well have been several further fund launches. Significant among recent newcomers is Standard Life which is almost certainly the largest pension fund manager in Europe. Also, because of the steady procession of mergers and take-overs that are currently changing the shape of the financial services industry, some funds are changing their names. For instance, what were Sun Life funds have become Axa Sun Life funds and the formerly named Merchant Investors funds have become part of the Lincoln stable. Some investment management groups such as Fidelity, Henderson and Jupiter sometimes manage funds on behalf of other companies as well as their own funds. Equally, the IFAs listed may have changed since the list was compiled with some moving into this specialist area of advice and, possibly, others leaving it as part of a merger, take-over or retirement process. However, none of this is exclusive to socially accountable investment and so these changes no more affect socially concerned investors than they do any others.

For the above reasons it is necessary to qualify the following directory and tables as being correct at the time of writing or compilation. If, by this stage, you are sufficiently motivated to wish to delve further into the possibilities of making your views felt in the world through the powerful medium of how you invest your money, then you could contact the Ethical Investment Research Service (EIRIS) or the UK Social Investment Forum (UKSIF) and subscribe to their regular newsletters and reports which will enable you to be fully up to date with developments in this growing investment sector. Equally, you may like to contact the companies or IFAs listed. This book does not seek to offer advice on what you should do but in the matter of how to invest (*see* Chapter 5) you should only go it alone and contact companies directly if you are looking for background material or if you are already an experienced and competent investor in your own right. Otherwise, you would be better tapping the experience and skills of an Independent Financial Adviser (IFA) to help you analyze your present financial circumstances, organize your own thoughts on where you would like to go (financially speaking) in the future, what you can afford now, what you will be able to afford in the likeliest future scenario and then find the most appropriate opportunities to match your objectives and priorities.

As far as IFAs are concerned, there is currently no requirement that they should ask a potential investor's ethical preferences when completing a fact-find (the starting document upon which IFAs base advice to clients). However, there are moves afoot to change this situation. The old adage is that 'if you don't ask, you won't get' but it might equally be said that if you are not informed, then you will be unable to ask. Many would say that knowing a potential investor's attitude to ethical issues is integral to knowing the client. The UK Social Investment Forum has been backed by the all-party parliamentary group on socially responsible investment in its call for questions about attitudes towards ethical investment to be included in the fact-find under the 'know your client' and 'best advice' rules that are part of the regulatory structure in the financial services industry, along with the other questions to establish who the investor is, and what are their needs and their attitude to risk. UKSIF conducts seminars around the country to inform the increasing number of IFAs who wish to add this dimension to their service. More than a third of IFAs questioned in a 1998 poll conducted by Friends Provident felt that ethical and green investment will become more important to their business over the next five years while only one in 50 thought that the issue would become less important.

Also, the appointment in October 1997 of a leading IFA in the ethical investment sector, Amanda Davidson, partner at IFA Holden Meehan, to the board of the Personal Investment Authority (PIA) suggests that the matter of ethics in investment is coming to the fore.

Criteria in summary

Tables 11.1 and 11.2 illustrate in a simplified form the avoidance and support criteria that different fund management teams have established in order to define the ethical and environmental priorities to which they refer when selecting a stock. These criteria are published in considerable detail by each of the investment management teams in the prospectus for their funds. Also, they publish lists of the stocks that they hold at any time. However, most investors will not have the means to judge the extent to which the stocks held conform to a fund's stated ethical and environmental criteria. Fortunately, there are very detailed versions of the information available from EIRIS in the publication *Money and Ethics* which is largely devoted to this aspect of ethical investment and is updated each year. EIRIS also offer a regular newsletter to subscribers which covers ethical investment and the issues which surround the subject. Ethical and Environmental Screening Services of Cheltenham also operate a regularly updated, PC-based screening service which considers the actual investments of the funds as well as the criteria they have published. Both services are valued by fund managers who are usually open to any information about the companies whose stock they hold on behalf of investors.

The ten areas listed in Table 11.1 (support criteria) may not seem many but remember that, until quite recently, ethical and environmental concerns were more likely to be expressed as rejection of activities deemed unethical or ecologically harmful than through support of activities seen as promoting positive values. However, nowadays, socially concerned investors are coming round to the view that it is as important to support the good as to boycott the bad. Indeed, some are now taking the view that they should invest in businesses deemed unethical or whose activities seem to damage the environment and, from that platform, campaign within the business for changes which will bring it up to best practice for its commercial sector. The emergence of a significant sector of businesses to support reflects a growing maturity and realism among socially responsible investors. This, in turn, is broadening the front on which fund managers may work and is moving socially responsible criteria into the mainstream of investment practice.

Table 11.1 is taken from *Financial Director* magazine (December 1997 issue). The information will be of value in sorting out those funds that seem to match most closely the priorities of an individual investor and, if used in combination with the fund selection suggestions in Chapter 5 (*see* Figures 5.1 and 5.2), will assist in the task of setting out concerns and matching them clearly with one or more of the various funds on offer. Tables 11.2 and 11.3 give financial details for funds and information about products available.

The next step

You should by now have a greater understanding of the whys, wherefores and hows of ethical investment together with all of its associated investment systems concerned with the environment and other aspects of the human condition under the general banner of socially responsible investments. Better still, you may now wish to go ahead and, with some of the savings and funds at your disposal, let those seeking investment funds know what it is that you care about and how you would prefer to see businesses run. That is as far as this book can take you. Why? Because, from here on, any steps you take must consider not only the priorities of the investment but also your own priorities as the investor and, as we saw at the beginning of the book, no two investors are the same. You will all have different needs and personal plans. However, there is a profession whose members study and qualify to guide and advise investors on just these matters.

Financial Advisers will know how to help their clients crystallize and prioritize their own financial requirements, how to reconcile these requirements to the financial resources available and then how to establish a plan to fulfil those requirements within those resources. Advisers fall broadly into three groups: those who work for the fund management companies (usually called company representatives); those who are contracted to but not employed by one company (usually called tied agents); and those who are completely independent of any company and are able to select the most appropriate product from the market to match their client's requirements as closely as possible (usually called Independent Financial Advisers or IFAs). Because all groups are governed by a strict code of practice established by the industry regulators, they are obliged to offer 'best advice' on the investment or savings vehicle which best fulfils the investor's financial aims. However, not all advisers specialize in the field of socially accountable investment although there is a growing campaign to include in the fact-find, on which advisers base their recommendations, a question about ethical or environmental concerns which the investor may wish to include among the criteria on which investment selection is to be based.

The following lists compiled by the Ethical Investment Research Service (EIRIS) and the UK Social Investment Forum (UKSIF) are of IFAs who have declared that they will introduce the dimension of ethical and environmental priorities to prospective savers and investors and will discuss this specialist field with them. The lists were correct at the time of publication (1999) but by the time you read this, an increasing number of IFAs may have extended their service to include the ethical and environmental dimension of investment. Also, while IFAs on these lists will include an ethical dimension in their service, that does not mean that IFAs not on the list will not include that dimension. UKSIF is promoting this view in the investment adviser community. You may well prefer to approach an IFA who is more local to you or with whom you have had previously satisfactory dealings, which is fine but, if you do, ask a few questions to ascertain the extent of their knowledge and experience of ethical and environmental investments. However, at the end of the day, if you know of some funds that can match your needs then ask the IFA to work within that group in order to find an appropriate investment. He or she will note for future reference that you limited the scope of any search for appropriate investments (the regulators require that) but will still be obliged to seek the best option within your chosen range.

The list of fund management groups which offer socially responsible funds was also correct at the time of writing but there may be new groups in this market by the time that you read these words. The summary of ethical funds indicates the relative ages and sizes of different funds at the time of writing. While it indicates how strong the sector has become and the fact that it is now a mainstream investment option, age and size will not be very important considerations when selecting a fund as the fund management businesses themselves will almost always be large and established enterprises with all of the strength that brings.

There remains only one thing for you to do: go and make a difference by making your feelings known in the clearest language of all – let your money talk, because the evidence suggests that it will be heard and it will make a difference.

Table 11.1
WHAT FUNDS TO SUPPORT AND WHAT FUNDS TO AVOID

The fund will avoid investing in companies that make, sell or exploit

The fund will invest in companies that actively promote

Fund	Weapons	Nuclear power/processing	Alcohol/tobacco	Pornography	Gambling	Animal cruelty	Human rights/oppressive regime	Ozone depleting chemicals or p	Environmentally damaging production	Fur/hardwood production	Pollution (air/waste)	Banking	Irresponsible marketing/advertising	Meat	Social/Community issues	Environmental protection/pollution control	Clean fuel/energy efficiency	Recycling/energy conservation	Healthcare/medical technology	Charitable giving	Positive employment practices	Safety and security	Training and education	Good corporate governance
1 Abbey Life Ethical Trust	X	X	X	X	X	X			X						✓				✓	✓			✓	
2 Abtrust Ethical Fund	X	X	X	X	X	X		X	X						✓					✓				
3 Allchurches Amity Fund		X	X	X	X	X									✓					✓				
4 CIS Environ Trust	X		X	X	X	X									✓				✓					
5 City Financial Acorn Eth Tst	X		X	X	X	X			X						✓									
6 Clerical Medical Evergreen Tst	X																							
7 Credit Suisse Fellowship Tst	X																							
8 CU Environmental Trust	X																							
9 Eagle Star Environ'l Opp Tst	X	X	X	X	X	X	X	X	X						✓	✓								
10 Equitable Ethical Trust	X	X	X	X	X	X	X		X			X			✓	✓			✓	✓	✓			✓
11 Ethical Investment Fund	X	X	X	X	X	X	X		X	X	X	X			✓	✓	✓	✓	✓		✓			
12 Framlington Health Fund	X	X	X	X	X	X									✓				✓	✓				
13 Fr Prov Ethical Investment Trust	X	X	X	X	X	X	X	X	X	X		X			✓	✓	✓	✓		✓	✓	✓	✓	✓
14 FP Inst'l Exempt UK Equity Tst[1]	X	X	X	X	X	X	X	X	X	X		X			✓	✓	✓	✓		✓	✓	✓	✓	✓
15 Fr Prov Stewardship Inc Tst	X		X	X	X	X	X	X	X	X		X			✓	✓	✓	✓	✓	✓	✓	✓	✓	✓
16 Fr Prov Stewardship Unit Trust	X		X	X	X	X	X	X	X	X		X			✓	✓	✓	✓	✓	✓	✓	✓	✓	✓

Table 11.1 cont.

	The fund will avoid investing in companies that make, sell or exploit														The fund will invest in companies that actively promote									
	Weapons	Nuclear power/processing	Alcohol/tobacco	Pornography	Gambling	Animal cruelty	Human rights/oppressive regime	Ozone depleting chemicals or p	Environmentally damaging practice	Fur/hardwood production	Pollution (air/waste)	Banking	Irresponsible marketing/advertising	Meat	Social/Community issues	Environmental protection/pollution control	Clean fuel/energy efficiency	Recycling/energy conservation	Healthcare/medical technology	Charitable giving	Positive employment practices	Safety and security	Training and education	Good corporate governance
17 Henderson Ethical Fund	X	X	X	X	X	X	X	X	X		X	X			✓	✓	✓			✓	✓		✓	✓
18 HFS Green Chip Fund	X	X	X	X			X		X						✓	✓				✓		✓		
19 Jupiter Ecology Fund	X	X	X												✓									
20 Jupiter Int'l Green Inv. Trust	X	X	X												✓									
21 Merchant Inv. Assur Eth Fund	X	X	X	X	X	X	X		X	X	X	X			✓									
22 NPI Global Care Inc Unit Tst	X	X	X	X	X	X	X		X	X	X	X			✓	✓	✓	✓	✓	✓	✓	✓	✓	✓
23 NPI Global Care Unit Trust	X	X	X	X	X	X	X		X	X	X	X			✓	✓	✓	✓	✓	✓	✓	✓	✓	✓
24 NPI Pension Global Care Mgd Fund[2]	X	X	X	X	X	X	X		X	X	X	X			✓	✓	✓	✓	✓	✓	✓	✓	✓	✓
25 NPI Pension Global Care[2]	X	X	X	X	X	X	X		X	X	X	X			✓	✓	✓	✓	✓	✓	✓	✓	✓	✓
26 Scottish Equitable Ethical Unit Trust	X	X	X	X	X	X									✓									
27 Soverign Ethical Fund	X	X	X	X	X		X	X	X	X	X	X			✓					✓	✓		✓	
28 Sun Life Global Port Ecol Fund	X						X		X	X					✓	✓								
29 TSB Environmental Inv Fund						X	X		X	X					✓	✓	✓			✓				
30 United Charities Ethical Trust	X	X												X	✓	✓								

* These are general categories. For a detailed explanation of ethical policies, contact EIRiS or the funds direct.
[1] Information from fund reports.
[2] Largest investments only

Source: Ethical criteria compiled by *Financial Director* using data on fund policy statements in *Money & Ethics*, published by EIRiS, 1997.

Table 11.2
SUMMARY OF ETHICAL FUNDS

Name of fund	Date of launch	Size at June 98
Abbey Life Ethical Trust	Sept 87	£48.6m
Aberdeen Prolific Ethical Unit Fund	Sept 92	£6.9m
Acorn Ethical Unit Trust	Dec 89	£5.2m
Albert E Sharp Ethical Fund	Mar 98	£1.7m
Allchurches Amity Fund	Mar 98	£38.1m
AXA Sun Life Ethical Fund	May 98	£0.9m
Barchester Best of Green Life Fund	Jun 91	£9.4m
Barchester Best of Green Offshore	Nov 93	£0.5m
Barchester Best of Green Pension Fund	Jun 91	£1.3m
CIS Environ Trust	May 90	£159.5m
CU Environmental Trust	Apr 92	£28.6m
Clerical Medical Evergreen Trust	Feb 90	£23.4m
Co-operative Bank Ethical Unit Trust	Nov 93	£17.3m
Credit Suisse Fellowship Trust	Jul 86	£99.1m
Equitable Ethical Trust	Jan 94	£19.7m
Ethical Investment Fund	Jan 86	£1.7m
Friends Provident Ethical Investment Trust	Dec 93	£36.7m
Friends Provident Stewardship Income Trust	Oct 87	£79.1m
Friends Provident Stewardship International Fund	Mar 98	£11.0m
Friends Provident Stewardship Pension Fund	Jun 84	£440.8m
Friends Provident Stewardship Unit Trust	Jun 84	£525.3m
FPAM Institutional Exempt Ethical UK Equity Trust	Oct 96	£74.9m
Framlington Health Fund	Apr 87	£88.7m
HFS Green Chip Fund	Nov 89	£15.8m
Henderson Ethical Fund	Feb 95	£30.4m
Jupiter Ecology Fund	Mar 88	£68.0m
Jupiter International Green Investment Trust	Dec 89	£46.0m
Merchant Investors Assurance Ethical Fund	Aug 95	£1.5m
NPI Global Care Income Unit Trust	Jul 95	£24.6m
NPI Global Care Unit Trust	Aug 91	£78.8m
NPI Pension Global Care	Mar 94	£30.1m
NPI Pension Global Care Managed Fund	Mar 96	£4.6m
Scottish Equitable Ethical Care Fund	Sept 98	£0.6m
Scottish Equitable Ethical Unit Trust (inc. Pension Fund)	Apr 89	£103.7m
Sovereign Ethical Fund	May 89	£24.5m
Standard Life UK Ethical Fund	Feb 98	£11m
Standard Life Ethical Fund	Feb 98	£9.7m
Sun Life Global Portfolio Ecological Fund	Dec 92	£10.4m
TSB Environmental Investor Fund	Jun 89	£23.0m
United Charities Ethical Trust	Feb 96	£10.3m
	Total	£2.2bn

Source: © EIRIS 1998

Robert Fleming have not provided details for the Oasis Fund (a fund launched for Islamic investors), so this fund cannot be analyzed. The Banner Real Life Fund and the NPI Social Index were launched after October 1998.

Table 11.3
PRODUCTS AVAILABLE FROM EACH FUND

Name of fund	Lump sum	Monthly savings	Life assurance	Personal pension	House purchase	PEP	Free Standing AVC's
AXA Sun Life Ethical Unit Trust	✓	✓	✓	✓	✓	✓	
Abbey Life Ethical Trust	✓	✓	✓	✓	✓	✓	✓
Aberdeen Prolific Ethical Unit Trust	✓	✓				✓	
Acorn Ethical Unit Trust	✓	✓		✓		✓	
Albert E Sharp Ethical PEP	✓		✓		✓	✓	
Albert E Sharp Ethical Unit Trust	✓					✓	
Allchurches Amith Fund	✓	✓		✓		✓	
Barchester Best of Green Life Fund	✓	✓	✓	✓			✓
Barchester Best of Green Offshore	✓	✓	✓	✓			✓
Barchester Best of Green Pension Fund	✓	✓	✓	✓			
CIS Environ Trust	✓					✓	✓
CU Environmental Trust	✓					✓	
Clerical Medical Evergreen Trust	✓	✓	✓	✓	✓	✓	✓
Co-operative Bank Ethical Unit Trust	✓						
Credit Suisse Fellowship Trust	✓	✓	✓			✓	
Equitable Ethical Trust	✓	✓	✓	✓		✓	
Ethical Investment Fund	✓		✓	✓	✓		
Ethical Investors Group Cruelty Free Fund *	✓	✓		✓	✓		
EP Ethical Investment Trust	✓	✓				✓	
FP Stewardship Income Trust	✓	✓				✓	✓
FP Stewardship International Trust	✓	✓				✓	

Table 11.3 cont.

Name of fund	Lump sum	Monthly savings	Life assurance	Personal pension	House purchase	PEP	Free Standing AVC's
FP Stewardship Life Fund[1]	✓	✓	✓		✓		
FP Stewardship Pension Fund	✓	✓		✓	✓		
FP Stewardship Unit Trust	✓	✓				✓	✓
FPAM Institutional Exempt Ethical UK Equity Trust	✓						
Framlington Health Fund	✓	✓				✓	✓
Genesis Capital Growth PEP *	✓	✓			✓	✓	
Genesis International Bond *	✓					✓	
Genesis Life PEP *	✓				✓	✓	✓
HFS Green Index Fund	✓	✓	✓			✓	
Henderson Ethical	✓	✓				✓	
Jupiter Ecology Fund	✓	✓				✓	
Jupiter International Green Inv. Trust	✓	✓					
Lincoln Green Fund *	✓	✓	✓	✓	✓	✓	✓
Merchant Investors Ethical CM Fund	✓		✓	✓			✓
Minerva Green Portfolio *	✓			✓		✓	
Minerva Green Switch Portfolio *	✓	✓		✓			
NPI Global Care Income Unit Trust	✓	✓				✓	
NPI Global Care Unit Trust	✓					✓	
NPI Pension Global Care	✓			✓			
NPI Pension Global Care Managed Fund	✓			✓			✓
NPI Life Global Care Fund	✓		✓				✓
NPI Life Global Care Managed Fund	✓		✓				✓

Table 11.3 cont.

Name of fund	Lump sum	Monthly savings	Life assurance	Personal pension	House purchase	PEP	Free Standing AVC's
Scottish Equitable Ethical Care Fund	✓	✓	✓				✓
Scottish Equitable Ethical Pension Fund²	✓	✓		✓	✓		✓
Scottish Equitable Ethical Unit Trust	✓	✓	✓			✓	
Skandia Ethical Managed Fund *	✓	✓	✓	✓		✓	✓
Sovereign Ethical Fund	✓	✓			✓	✓	
Standard Life UK Ethical Fund	✓	✓			✓	✓	
Standard Life Pension Ethical Fund	✓	✓		✓		✓	✓
Sun Life Global Portfolio Ecological Fund	✓	✓	✓	✓			✓
TSB Environmental Investor Fund	✓		✓				
United Charities Ethical Trust	✓	✓				✓	

* These are fund of funds. Before investing in a fund of funds investors should check not only its ethical policy but also those of all the other ethical funds.

Source: © EIRIS 1998

INDEPENDENT FINANCIAL ADVISERS WHO OFFER ADVICE ON ETHICAL INVESTMENT

....

This list has been produced based on an original list from EIRIS. IFAs are included by EIRIS if, in 1997, they put more than £100,000 of business in ethical funds or put more than 40 per cent of their business in ethical funds or bought the EIRIS guide *Choosing an Ethical Fund* in 1998.

Firms that subscribe to the EIRIS guide *Choosing an Ethical Fund* are marked with an asterisk (*).

The Personal Investment Authority (PIA) is the regulatory body for most firms conducting investment business with the private investor. The PIA deals with any complaints about IFAs. EIRIS shows this list annually to the PIA and passes any complaints received concerning these IFAs to the PIA. IFAs are only included on this list if they are authorized to give financial advice by the PIA or a recognized professional body, or if they are an approved representative of a Network. EIRIS has verified that the named individuals are registered with the PIA or a recognized professional body.

Peer Allatson Financial Management*
3rd Floor, Kimberley House, 47 Vaughan Way, Leicester LE1 4SG
Main contact: Peter Allatson
Qualifications of contact: FPC
Tel: 0116 251 6100 *Fax:* 0116 253 6768
E-mail: prsa@netcomuk.co.uk

Arbuthnot Pensions & Investments (Exeter)
22 Southernhay West, Exeter, Devon EX1 1PR
Main contact: Tim Aggett
Qualifications of contact: FPC
Tel: 01392 410 080 *Fax:* 01392 413 638

Amherst Financial Services Ltd*
Somerset House, Clarendon Place, Leamington Spa, Warks CV32 5QN
Main contact: Kenneth Lines
Qualifications of contact: FPC + (D)
Tel: 01926 431 314 *Fax:* 01926 431 315
Appointed representative of DBS Financial Management PLC

Barchester Green Investment*
45–49 Catherine Street, Salisbury, Wiltshire SP1 2DH
Main contact: Rodney Palmer
Qualifications of contact: FPC
Tel: 01722 331 241 *Fax:* 01722 414 191
E-mail: info@barchestergreen.co.uk

Blackfriars Financial Services Ltd*
6 Congleton Road, Sandbach, Cheshire CW11 1HN
Main contact: Edward Stott
Qualifications of contact: FPC + (B)
Tel: 01270 762 656 *Fax:* 01270 768 259
Appointed representative of Burns Anderson Independent Network

Blackstone Franks Financial Management Ltd*
26–34 Old Street, London EC1V 9HL
Main contact: Gary Treen
Qualifications of contact: FPC (+A, E)
Tel: 0171 336 1111 *Fax:* 0171 336 1100

D.L. Bloomer & Partners*
53 Bothwell Street, Glasgow G2 6TS
Main contact: Keith L Muir
Qualifications of contact: FPC
Tel: 0141 248 7268 *Fax:* 0141 221 2475
E-mail: D2266611@infotrade.co.uk

BMP Financial Services*
52 Station Road, Egham, Surrey TW20 9LF
Main contact: Colin Carter
Qualifications of contact: FPC + (E)
Tel: 01784 433 679 *Fax:* 01784 431 839

Bromige and Partners
22 Hartfield Road, Forest Row, East Sussex RH18 5DY
Main contact: Christian Thal-Jantzen
Qualifications of contact: FPC
Tel: 01342 826703 *Fax:* 01342 826704
Other contact: David Bromige
Qualification: FPC
Tel/Fax: 0171 384 1578
E-mail: invest@bromige-partners.demon.co.uk

Castle Investment Consultants*
19–21 Junction Road, Totton, Southampton, Hants SO40 9HG
Main contact: David Foot
Qualifications of contact: FPC
Tel: 01703 873 187 *Fax:* 01703 863 222
E-mail: David.Foot@btinternet.com

Chadwick Financial Management Ltd*
Chadwick House, Hauley Road, Dartmouth, Devon TQ6 9AA
Main contact: Michael R Cooper
Qualifications of contact: FPC + (C, E)
Tel: 01803 834 440 *Fax:* 01803 835 641

CCF Financial Services Ltd*
8 Mill Road, Cambridge CB1 2AD
Main contact: John Abraham
Qualifications of contact: FPC
Tel: 01223 354 354 *Fax:* 01223 460 554
E-mail: ccf@dial.pipex.com

Chapter House Investments*
North Muskham Prebend, Church Street, Southwell, Nottinghamshire
   NG25 0HQ
Main contact: Michael P Dixon
Qualifications of contact: FPC
Tel: 01636 816 922
E-mail: chapter1@ifa.net
Member of IFA Network Ltd

Chew Valley Financial Services*
Woodlands, Chew Hill, Chew Magna, Bristol BS18 8SA
Main contact: Colin Beaven
Qualifications of contact: FPC
Tel: 01275 333 795 *Fax:* 01275 333 745
Appointed representative of DBS Financial Management PLC

Citywall Financial Management Ltd*
12 Bedford Street, Exeter, Devon EX1 1LG
Main contact: Michael Harrison
Qualifications of contact: FPC
Tel: 01392 422 592 *Fax:* 01392 495 441
E-mail: Citywallfm@aol.com

Coggans Wood & Co.
61 Manor Place, Edinburgh EH3 7EG
Main contact: Jackie Smith
Qualifications of contact: FPC + (D)
Tel: 0131 225 7777 *Fax:* 0131 220 1016
E-mail: cwcedin@aol.com
Also at Kirkaldy, *tel:* 01592 267 151

Coracle Financial Services Ltd*
Broadway House, 2 Haygate Road, Wellington, Telford TF1 1QA
Main contact: Brian L Banks
Qualifications of contact: FPC + (A, C, D)
Tel: 01952 245 235 *Fax:* 01952 245 777
Appointed representative of Berkeley Independent Advisers Ltd

The County Partnership*
Charter House, 31 St George's Road, Cheltenham, Gloucestershire GL50 3DU
Main contact: Henry Hodgkins
Qualifications of contact: FPC
Tel: 01242 253 136 *Fax:* 01242 253 025
E-mail: henry@countypartnership.co.uk
Appointed representative of Countrywide Independent Advisers Ltd

Cranwell Investments Ltd*
3 Mill House, Carre Street, Sleaford, Lincs NG34 7TW
Main contact: Greville Price
Qualifications of contact: FPC
Tel: 01529 360 040 *Fax:* 01529 306 050
E-mail: info@cranwell.co.uk

Crowe Money Advice*
69 Jamestown Road, London NW1 7DB
Main contact: John Crowe
Qualifications of contact: FPC
Tel: 0171 485 9738 *Fax:* 0171 482 3184

Direct Independent Financial Consultants*
Parker Court, St James Square, Cheltenham, Gloucestershire GL51 3QJ
Main contact: Forrest Wheeler
Qualifications of contact: FPC
Tel: 01242 253 339 *Fax:* 01242 241 532
Appointed representative of Berkeley Independent Advisers Ltd

Ethical Financial
7–8 Ty Verlon Business Park, Barry, South Glamorgan CF63 2BE
Main contact: Brian Spence
Qualifications of contact: FPC
Tel: 01446 421 123 *Fax:* 01446 421 478
E-mail: ethical@ethical-financial.co.uk
Other contact: Keith Jenkyns
Tel: 01446 421 123
Qualifications: FPC
Regulated by Personal Investment Authority

Ethical Investments*
955a Ecclesall Road, Sheffield S11 8TN
Main contact: David Vincent
Qualifications of contact: FPC
Tel: 0114 266 7400 *Fax:* 0114 268 2248
E-mail: dvincent@ethicalinvestments.co.uk
Appointed representative of DBS Financial Management PLC

Ethical Investors Group
Greenfield House, Guiting Power, Cheltenham GL54 5TZ
Main contact: Lee Coates
Qualifications of contact: FPC + (A, E, D)
Tel: 01451 850 777 *Fax:* 01451 850 705
Web: www.oneworld.org/ethical-investors

The Ethical Investment Co-operative Ltd*
39 Exchange Street, Norwich, Norfolk NR2 1DP
Main contact: Alan Kirkham
Qualifications of contact: FPC
Tel: 01603 661 121 *Fax:* 01603 621 123
Freephone: 0800 731 9259
E-mail: EIC@IFA.net
Other contact: Ian Harland (Darlington Office)
Qualifications: FPC
Tel: 01325 267 229 *Fax:* 01325 267 200
E-mail: greeninvest@gn.apc.org
Other contact: Guy Hooker (Edinburgh Office)
Qualifications: FPC
Tel: 0131 466 4666 *Fax:* 0131 466 4667
E-mail: ethicalmoney@gn.apc.org
Other contact: Peter Liebich (Shrewsbury Office)
Qualifications: FPC
Tel/Fax: 01743 343 800
E-mail: ethically@IFA.net

The Ethical Partnership*
146 Bournemouth Road, Chandlers Ford, Eastleigh, Hampshire SO53 3AL
Main contact: Jeremy Newbegin
Qualifications of contact: FPC
Tel: 01703 361361 *Fax:* 01703 365364
E-mail: J.newbegin@mcmail.com
Notes: Freephone Enquiry Line: 0800 092 4090

Ethikos Independent Financial Advisers*
816 Oxford Road, Reading RG30 1EL
Main contact: Peter J Chesworth
Qualifications of contact: FPC
Tel: 0118 958 6998 *Fax:* 0118 958 6998
Appointed representative of The Kestrel Network

Everett MacLeod Limited*
35 Paul Street, London EC2A 4JU
Main contact: Mike MacLeod
Qualifications of contact: FPC + (A, B)
Tel: 0171 628 0857 *Fax:* 0171 628 7253
E-mail: money@everettmac.co.uk
A member of DBS Financial Management PLC which is regulated by the
    Personal Investment Authority

Fleetwood MAC (Money Advice Consultants) Ethical Investment Shop*
Cragg Cottage, Garnett Bridge, Kendal LA8 9AZ
Main contact: John Fleetwood
Qualifications of contact: FPC
Tel: 01539 823 041 *Fax:* 01539 823 041
E-mail: info@bannergroup.com
Appointed representative of DBS Financial Management PLC

Fleming Associates
Albion Court, 1 Pierce Street, Macclesfield, Cheshire SK11 6ER
Main contact: Ms E. Fleming
Qualifications of contact: FPC + (B)
Tel: 01625 611 791 *Fax:* 01625 611 791

GÆIA – Global and Ethical Investment Advice*
Investment House, 425 Wilmslow Road, Manchester M20 4AF
Main contact: Brigid Benson
Qualifications of contact: FPC
Tel: 0161 434 4681 *Fax:* 0161 445 8421
E-mail: brigid@gaeia.u-net.com
Notes: GAEIA acquired the businesses of Green Door Associates and Tree
    of Life in 1997

R C Gray & Co Ltd*
2B Church Street, Wedmore, Somerset BS28 4AB
Main contact: Mark Meldon
Qualifications of contact: FPC
Tel: 01934 713 227 *Fax:* 01934 713 373
E-mail: RobinGray@email.msn.com

H & M Independent Financial Advisers
9 Cotwall End Road, Lower Gornal, Dudley, West Midlands DY3 3ER
Main contact: Howard Simpson
Qualifications of contact: FPC
Tel: 0800 018 4791 *Fax:* 01384 234 791
E-mail: info@hmifas.infotrade.co.uk
Web: http://www.businessfile.com/hmifas/
Appointed Representative of DBS Financial Management PLC

Holden Meehan*
11th Floor, Clifton Heights, Triangle West, Clifton, Bristol BS8 1EJ
Main contact: Pat Meehan
Qualifications of contact: FPC
Tel: 0117 925 2874 *Fax:* 0117 929 1535
E-mail: pmeehan@holdenm.demon.co.uk
Other contact: Richard Hunter (London office)
Qualifications: FPC
Tel: 0171 692 1700 *Fax:* 0171 692 1701

IFA Plus*
8 Portswood Park, Southampton, Hampshire SO17 2EW
Main contact: John Donaldson
Qualifications of contact: FPC
Tel: 01703 905 825 *Fax:* 01703 779 769
Appointed representative of IFA Network Ltd

Independent Insurance Advisers (Cheltenham) Ltd*
19 Horsefair, Chipping Norton, Oxon OX7 5AL
Main contact: Mark Dancer
Qualifications of contact: FPC
Tel: 01608 641 200 *Fax:* 01608 641 186

The Investment Practice
Suite 4, The Sanctuary, 23 Oakhill Grove, Surbiton, Surrey KT6 6DU
Main contact: Dominic Thomas
Qualifications of contact: FPC
Tel: 0181 339 9444 *Fax:* 0181 339 9555
E-mail: dominic@tip.uk.com

Key Services Ltd*
Loan House, 10 The Loan, South Queensferry EH30 9NS
Main contact: David W Yorke
Qualifications of contact: FPC
Tel: 0131 331 5555   *Fax:* 0131 331 5455
E-mail: advice@ksl-uk.com
Notes: *Web:* http://www.ksl-uk.com

Kingswood Consultants*
Kingswood House, 29 North Street, Bicester, Oxon OX6 7NB
Main contact: Mike Daniels
Qualifications of contact: FPC
Tel: 01869 252 545   *Fax:* 01869 240 759
E-mail: mikedaniels@kingswoodethical.co.uk
Web: www.kingswoodethical.co.uk.

Lifestyle Financial Services Ltd*
13 Wright Street, Kingston upon Hull, East Yorkshire HU2 8HU
Main contact: Mike Robertson
Qualifications of contact: FPC
Tel: 01482 217 234   *Fax:* 01482 219 426
E-mail: ifa@lifestyle.karoo.co.uk
Notes: *Web:* http://www.karoo.net/lifestyle
Provide quarterly Ethical Investment seminars

Lupton Fawcett*
Yorkshire House, Greek Street, Leeds LS1 5SX
Main contact: John Eaton
Qualifications of contact: FPC + (D)
Tel: 0113 280 2000   *Fax:* 0113 280 2163

Murray Borrill & Partners*
Moorgate House, 23 Moorgate Road, Rotherham S60 2EN
Main contact: Julian Crooks
Qualifications of contact: FPC + (A, D)
Tel: 01709 371 675   *Fax:* 01709 371 735
E-mail: mbfinser@globalnet.co.uk
Appointed representative of IFA Network Ltd

Ivan Massow Associates*
18 Mortimer Street, London W1N 7RD
Main contact: Sarah Killick
Qualifications of contact: FPC + (A)
Tel: 0171 631 1111   *Fax:* 0171 631 0111
E-mail: Appointed representative of DBS Financial Management PLC

Millbrae Financial Services Ltd
46 Millbrae Road, Glasgow G42 9TU
Main contact: Carl Melvin
Qualifications of contact: FPC + (A, B, C, D)
Tel: 0141 649 0000 *Fax:* 0141 632 9988
E-mail: info@millbrae.co.uk

Money Matters
83 Victoria Road, Cambridge CB4 3BS
Main contact: Stephen Clifton
Qualifications of contact: FPC
Tel: 01223 312 203 *Fax:* 01223 576 866
E-mail: money.mattes@dial.pipex.com

PolicySales Limited*
4 Oak Tree Place, Manaton Close, Exeter EX2 8WA
Main contact: Mike Crew
Qualifications of contact: FPC
Tel: 01392 203 686 *Fax:* 01392 824 132
E-mail: advice@ksl-uk.com
Appointed representative of First Financial Planning

Premier Investment Management Service*
Capital House, 36 Angle End, Great Wilbraham, Cambridge CB1 5JG
Main contact: Lance Sharman
Qualifications of contact: FPC + (D)
Tel: 01223 882 422 *Fax:* 01223 882 423
E-mail: pims@globalnet.co.uk

Rainbow Finance Limited
Elms Court, West Way, Botley, Oxford OX2 9LP
Main contact: Louis Letourneau
Qualifications of contact: FPC
Tel: 0800 328 0625/01865 727 227 *Fax:* 01865 243 377
E-mail: *postbox@rainbow-finance.com*
Appointed representative of Interlink Premier Network Ltd

Rainbow IFAs*
16 South Queen Street, Morley, Leeds LS27 9EW
Main contact: James Kenny
Qualifications of contact: FPC
Tel: 0113 238 1993 *Fax:* 0113 238 1994

Rhys Lewis IFA*
St John's House, 5 South Parade, Summertown, Oxford OX2 7JL
Main contact: Geoff Mason
Qualifications of contact: FPC
Tel: 01865 310 990 *Fax:* 01865 516 010
E-mail: mbfinser@globalnet.co.uk
Appointed representative of IFA Network Ltd

Diane Saunders
351 Harrogate Road, Leeds LS17 6PZ
Main contact: Diane Saunders
Qualifications of contact: FPC
Tel: 0113 268 9102 *Fax:* 0113 237 0695
Appointed representative of Countrywide Independent Advisers Ltd

Alan Seward Financial Services*
19 Gay Street, Bath BA1 2PD
Main contact: Michael Price/Jill Beavis
Qualifications of contact: FPC
Tel: 01225 448 832 *Fax:* 01225 448 835
E-mail: www.alanseward.co.uk
Appointed representative of Countrywide Independent Advisers Ltd

Shropshire Independent Financial & Mortgage Services*
Burnside House, Mill Road, Meole Brace, Shrewsbury SY3 9JT
Main contact: Mrs Rosemary Heaversedge
Qualifications of contact: FPC + (A, C, D)
Tel: 01743 364 381 *Fax:* 01743 368 488
Appointed representative of DBS Financial Management PLC

St Peter's*
The Meadows, Church Road, Dodleston, Chester CH4 9NG
Main contact: Colum Wilde
Qualifications of contact: FPC
Tel: 01244 660 640 *Fax:* 01244 660 641
E-mail: stpeters@compuserve.com

Stuart Brown & Associates*
Helm House, 1–3 Cranfield Place, London NW6 3BU
Main contact: Dominic Stuart
Qualifications of contact: FPC
Tel: 0171 372 5000 *Fax:* 0171 372 5552

Troy, French & Partners*
66 Alwyne Road, Wimbledon, London SW19 7AE
Main contact: Mike Troy
Qualifications of contact: AFPC
Tel: 0181 879 0802/1006 *Fax:* 0181 287 6677
Other contact: Peter French
Tel: 0181 879 0802
Qualifications: FPC (and A)
E-mail: troyfrench@cableinet.co.uk

David Walters Financial Services*
Horseshoe Cottage, Brownbread Street, Ashburnham, East Sussex TN33 9NX
Main contact: David Walters
Qualifications of contact: FPC + (E)
Tel: 01424 893 113 *Fax:* 01424 893 443
E-mail: davidwalters2@compuserve.com
Web: http://www.seven.net/moneyweb/dbs/tn339nx/index.html
Notes: Appointed representative of DBS Financial Management PLC

Westerby Investment Management
15 Andover Street, Leicester LE2 0JA
Main contact: Peter Clamp
Qualifications of contact: FPC
Tel: 0116 247 0304 *Fax:* 0116 247 1163

Wise Investment*
The Lectern Hall, West Street, Chipping Norton, Oxon OX7 5LH
Main contact: Tony Yarrow
Qualifications of contact: FPC
Tel: 01608 642 233 *Fax:* 01608 642 200
E-mail: wise@wiseinv.demon.co.uk

Woodstock Financial Services*
53 Whyteleafe Hill, Whyteleafe, Surrey CR3 0AJ
Main contact: Derek W Vivian
Qualifications of contact: FPC
Tel: 0181 763 1717 *Fax:* 0181 763 1717
E-mail: wfs@btinternet.com
Member of IFA Network Ltd

Ane Wray Independent Financial Adviser*
Old Chapel House, 3 Heapey Road, Little Knowlet, Chorley, Lancashire
   PR6 9BD
Main contact: Anne Wray
Qualifications of contact: FPC
Tel: 01257 233 023 *Fax:* 01257 268 751
E-mail: annewray@ifa.u-net.com
Appointed representative of DBS Financial Management PLC

DIRECTORY OF FUNDS

....

The following directory is taken from the membership list of the UK Social Investment Forum (UKSIF). While those who take the trouble to join such a group are clearly signalling their commitment to socially responsible investment, it does not mean that IFAs and investment managers who are not members are not committed to the same principles.

Or, if you do not have access to the internet, UKSIF may be contacted directly:

The Administrator
UK Social Investment Forum
Suite 308, 16 Baldwins Gardens, London EC1N 7RJ
Tel: 0171 404 1993 *Fax:* 0171 404 1994
E-mail: info@uksif.org *or* uksif@gn.apc.org

You may also contact the Ethical Investment Research Society (EIRIS). If you wish to order *Money and Ethics* or subscribe to other EIRIS services, you should call 0845 606 0324. For any other enquiries, the address is:

EIRIS Services Ltd
80–84 Bondway, London SW8 1SF
Tel: 0171 840 5700 *Fax:* 0171 735 5323
E-mail: ethics@eiris.win-uk.net

Directory of Members January 1999

The UK Social Investment Forum (UKSIF) publishes this directory of members as a marketing and outreach tool for itself and its members and as a resource guide for the interested public. The information listed is provided by the member and is not independently verified by UKSIF. The guide is updated regularly. Membership of UKSIF is open to individuals, businesses, charities, voluntary sector organizations, governmental and other organizations in the social investment and related fields. By joining UKSIF, members subscribe to the following statement of principles.

Statement of principles

1 Members agree to support the work of and to disseminate information about UKSIF and the work of its members.
2 Members commit to assist, either individually or with other UKSIF

members, in improving the public's understanding of Socially Responsible Investment and in supporting the theory and practice of SRI, including the concepts of ethical, socially directed, environmental and green investments.

3 Members endeavour to place the public interest and the interest of their clients over their own. The responsibility of UKSIF members extends not only to the individual, but to society.

4 Members strive to act with a high degree of personal integrity, maintaining honourable relationships with colleagues, clients, and all those who rely on the members' professional judgement and skills.

5 Members seek continually to maintain and improve the knowledge, skills and competence relevant to their profession and be diligent in the performance of their occupational duties.

6 Members make an affirmative commitment to apply honest, thorough and diligent methods of research and evaluation.

7 Members should obey the laws and regulations relevant to their profession and should avoid any conduct or activity that would cause unjust harm to others.

8 Members should use the fact of membership in a manner consistent with the UKSIF Statement of principles. Membership of UKSIF is not intended to endorse an individual member's or organization's business qualifications, values or practices.

Membership disclaimer

Membership of the UK Social Investment Forum is not intended to endorse an individual's or organization's business goals, values or practices and the UK Social Investment Forum assumes no legal or financial responsibility for the practices of the individuals or organizations listed as members.

Mission statement

The Forum's primary purpose is to promote and encourage the development and positive impact of Socially Responsible Investment (SRI) throughout the UK.

Socially Responsible Investment combines investors' financial objectives with their commitment to social concerns such as social justice, economic development, peace or a healthy environment.

Aims and objectives

1 To inform, educate and provide a forum for discussion and debate for our membership and the public at large about the issues and developments in the SRI field

2 To promote the understanding of Socially Responsible Investment and to

encourage the development of appropriate SRI practices and vehicles

3 To identify, encourage and help develop working models which demonstrate the effectiveness of SRI in alleviating social hardship, protecting and
   preserving the environment and stimulating sustainable economic
   development

4 To support and encourage a greater sense of social accountability amongst
   investors – both corporate financial institutions and individuals

5 To encourage and expect high ethical standards of professional conduct as
   outlined by the UKSIF statement of principles to which all members ascribe

6 To undertake and publish research for required changes in legislation and
   company policies and practices to enable SRI to develop rapidly and effectively in the UK and internationally

7 To promote co-operation with European and other international SRI
   organizations through the exchange of information and ideas.

Issued by the Directors of the UK Social Investment Forum, October 9 1990

INDEPENDENT FINANCIAL
ADVISERS

....

Balfour Finance IFAs
67–83 Shandwick Place, Edinburgh EH2 4SD
Contact: Rosemary Hunter
Tel: 0131 221 9060 *Fax:* 0131 221 1103

Banner Financial Services
Banner House, Church Road, Copthorne, Crawley RH10 3RA
Contact: David Alton
Tel: 01342 717 917 *Fax:* 01342 712 534
E-mail: info@bannergroup.com

Barchester Green Investment
Barchester House, 45–49 Catherine Street, Salisbury, Wiltshire SP1 2DH
Contact: Geoffrey Griffiths
Tel: 01722 331 241 *Fax:* 01722 414 191
E-mail: info@barchestergreen.co.uk

Bromige and Partners
22 Hartfield Road, Forest Row, East Sussex RH18 5DY
Contact: Christian Thal-Jantzen
Contact's title: Director
Tel: 01342 826 703 *Fax:* 01342 826 704
E-mail: invest@bromige-partners.demon.co.uk

Crowe Money Advice
69 Jamestown Road, London NW1 7DB
Contact: Mr John Crowe
Tel: 0171 485 9738 *Fax:* 0171 482 3184

Davies and Chapman
143 Stoke Newington Church Street, London N16 0UH
Contact: Ms Sarah Chapman
Tel: 0171 923 9069 *Fax:* 0171 923 9045

Ethical Investments
955a Ecclesall Road, Sheffield S11 8TN
Contact: David Vincent
Tel: 0114 266 7400 *Fax:* 0114 268 2248
E-mail: dvincent@ethicalinvestments.co.uk
Web: www.ethicalinvestments.co.uk

Ethical Investors Group
Greenfield House, Guiting Power, Cheltenham GL54 5TZ
Contact: Lee Coates
Tel: 01451 850 777 *Fax:* 01451 850 705
E-mail: ethics@gn.apc.org
Web: www.oneworld.org/ethical-investors/

Ethikos Independent Financial Advisers
816 Oxford Road, Reading RG30 1EL
Contact: Peter J Chesworth
Contact's title: Principal
Tel: 0118 958 6998 *Fax:* 0118 958 6998

Fleetwood MAC (Money Advice Consultants) Ethical Investment Shop
Cragg Cottage, Garnett Bridge, Kendal LA8 9AZ
Contact: John Fleetwood
Tel: 01539 823 041 *Fax:* 01539 823 041
E-mail: info@bannergroup.com

Global and Ethical Investment Advice (GAEIA)
Investment House, 425 Wilmslow Road, Manchester M20 4AF
Contact: Brigid Benson
Contact's title: Principal
Tel: 0161 434 4681 *Fax:* 0161 445 8421
E-mail: brigid@gaeia.u-net.com

Helm Financial Services Ltd
Helm House, 1–3 Canfield Place, London NW6 3BU
Contact: Dominic Stuart
Tel: 0171 372 5000 *Fax:* 0171 372 5552
E-mail: helmbob@aol.com

Holden Meehan
New Penderel House, 283–287 High Holborn, London WC1V 7HP
Contact: Amanda Davidson
Contact's title: Partner
Tel: 0171 692 1700 *Fax:* 0171 692 1701
E-mail: holdenm@holdenm.demon.co.uk

The Investment Practice
Suite 4, The Sanctuary, 23 Oakhill Grove, Surbiton, Surrey KT6 6DU
Contact: Dominic Thomas
Tel: 0181 339 9444 *Fax:* 0181 339 9555

K L Plester Financial Services Ltd
Cover House, 112–113 Bewdley Road, Kidderminster, Worcs DY11 6RX
Contact: Philip Powell
Contact's title: Director
Tel: 01562 829 898 *Fax:* 01562 746 089
E-mail: philip@glassworks.freeserve.co.uk

Kingswood Consultants
Kingswood House, 29 North Street, Bicester, Oxon OX6 7NB
Contact: Mike Daniels
Contact's title: Principal
Tel: 01869 252 545 *Fax:* 01869 240 759
E-mail: mikedaniels@kingswoodethical.co.uk
Web: www.kingswoodethical.co.uk

Lifestyle Financial Services Ltd
13 Wright Street, Kingston upon Hull, East Yorkshire HU2 8HU
Contact: Mike Robertson
Contact's title: Managing Director
Tel: 01482 217 234 *Fax:* 01482 219 426
E-mail: ifa@lifestyle.karoo.co.uk

Mark Armstrong Financial Services
8 Elstow Close, Over, Cambridge CB4 5LU
Contact: Mark Armstrong
Contact's title: Principal
Tel: 01954 231 049 *Fax:* 01954 231 049
E-mail: markarmst@aol.com

Rainbow Finance Limited
Elms Court, West Way, Botley, Oxford OX2 9LP
Contact: Louis Letourneau
Contact's title: Managing Director
Tel: 0800 328 0625/01865 727 227 *Fax:* 01865 243 377
E-mail: postbox@rainbow-finance.com

The Ethical Investment Co-operative
Vincent House, 15 Victoria Road, Darlington, Co Durham DL1 5SF
Contact: Guy Hooker
Contact's title: Director
Tel: 01325 267 228 *Fax:* 01325 267 200

Woodstock Financial Services
53 Whyteleafe Hill, Whyteleafe, Surrey CR3 0AJ
Contact: Derek W Vivian
Contact's title: Principal
Tel: 0181 763 1717 *Fax:* 0181 763 1717
E-mail: wfs@btinternet.com

In addition, all members of the Ethical Investment Association are members of the UK Social Investment Forum. Details from:

Ethical Investment Association
Garnett Bridge, Kendal LA8 9AZ
Contact: John Fleetwood
Tel: 01539 823 041 *Fax:* 01539 823 041
E-mail: john@fleetmac.infotrade.co.uk

INVESTMENT MANAGEMENT INSTITUTIONS

....

Axa Sun Life
Sun Life Centre, PO Box 1810, Bristol BS99 5SN
Contact: David Brickley
Contact's title: Investment Marketing Manager
Tel: 0117 989 9100 *Fax:* 0117 989 1810

Sun Life has long sought to follow an ethical and socially responsible investment policy while meeting the financial needs of our policyholders. We have now gone one step further with the launch of the Ethical fund, which is available across the full range of our products. The fund only invests in companies that meet a range of ethical criteria. We believe that investors are far more socially conscious now than ever before in the way they wish their savings to be invested and this trend is likely to continue.

Capel-Cure Sharp
Pinners Hall, 105–108 Old Broad Street, London EC2N 1ET
Contact: Fleur Leach
Contact's title: Head of Ethical Investment
Tel: 0171 638 7275 *Fax:* 0171 638 7270

Capel-Cure Sharp offers investors alternative investment opportunities that allow investment in companies that are responsible and committed to improving their business practices, with the introduction of an Ethical Unit and Investment Trust Service, bespoke Portfolio Management Service and Ethical Unit Trust.

CCLA Investment Management Ltd
St Alphage House, 2 Fore Street, London EC2Y 5AQ
Contact: Neville White
Contact's title: Senior Ethical Investment Researcher
Tel: 0171 588 1815 *Fax:* 0171 256 6333
E-mail: investment@ccla.co.uk

Established in 1987, CCLA Investment Management Ltd, regulated by IMRO, is a leading specialist investment management company serving charities, churches and local authorities. It currently provides investment services to institutional funds amounting to some £33.1 billion. As manager of the CFB Church of England Funds for parishes and dioceses, CCLA works in conjunction with the Church Commissioners for England and the Church of England Pension Board on the ethical investment policy of the central Church of England investment bodies.

CIS Unit Managers Ltd
Miller Street
Manchester M60 0AL
Contact: Mr R Taylor
Contact's title: Environmental Officer
Tel: 0161 837 4043 *Fax*: 0161 837 4048
E-mail: cis@cis.co.uk
Web: www.cis.co.uk

CIS Unit Managers operates three unit trusts of which one, the CIS Environ Trust, invests on the basis of predetermined positive criteria. In order to qualify, companies must be involved in enhancing the environment, human health or safety or engaged in activities considered in some way to improve quality of life. Companies selected on the positive criteria are then assessed to establish whether they are active in areas that the Trust seeks to avoid. These are concerned with animal testing, military applications, countries where human rights are disregarded, tobacco and the generation of nuclear power. Independent researchers screen companies for the Trust and an independent advisory committee reviews all companies considered and more general issues where there are areas of doubt or special circumstances. The approach is to weight the benefits of positive factors against other considerations in light of the information available.

Ecclesiastical Insurance Group
19–21 Billiter Street
London EC3M 2RY
Contact: Susan Round
Tel: 01452 528 533 *Fax*: 01452 423 577

Enterprise Ventures Ltd
Enterprise House
17 Ribblesdale Place
Preston PR1 3NA
Contact: Deborah Heyes
Contact's title: Investment Manager

Tel: 01772 203 020 *Fax*: 01772 880 697
E-mail: ventures@enterprise.co.uk

As such, EVL has, over the past four years, participated in the field of social investment, managing a £33m loan fund during that period. The fund provided loans to economically viable enterprises in England, supporting 'not for profit' projects for which traditional forms of funding were unavailable.

Family Assurance Friendly Society
16–17 West Street, Brighton BN1 2RL
Contact: Peter Atkins
Contact's title: IFA Sales Manager
Tel: 01273 725 272 *Fax*: 01273 206 026
E-mail: patkins@family.co.uk

Family offers a range of ethical products that invest in Family Assurance's Charities Ethical Trust. The trust was established in 1982 by Lord Rix and Mencap City Foundation and Family Investment Management (a wholly owned subsidiary of Family Assurance Friendly Society) became responsible for the management of the trust in 1993. In March 1996, after consultation with the charities on the Advisory Board, the investment objectives of the fund were changed to incorporate ethical criteria.

The portfolio of companies in Family Assurance's Charities Ethical Trust is reviewed frequently and we subscribe to EIRIS in order to ensure that companies chosen for the fund will pass our ethical criteria.

More recently, Family established an ethical sub committee to monitor and take forward the Family Assurance Ethical Trust Fund and to discuss issues relevant to ethical investment.

As a mutual organization, Family Assurance is committed to the advancement of socially responsible investment.

Friends Provident Life Office
15 Old Bailey, London EC4M 7AP
Contact: Craig Mackenzie
Contact's title: Ethics Unit Manager
Tel: 0171 506 1100 *Fax*: 0171 236 2060
E-mail: c.mackenzie@friendsprovident.co.uk

Friends Provident Life Office launched the UK's first ethical unit trust, life and pension fund range in June 1984, which was given the name 'Stewardship' by Charles Jacob MBE. The fund was the result of several years of searching for a solution that would best serve the needs of those members who did not consider the financial return to be the only reason for choosing an investment.

Friends Provident's Stewardship range of funds now includes UK, International and Managed fund options across a range of investment products. Ethically screened funds now total around £31 billion, most of which is within the Stewardship range.

Friends Provident sees the Ethical Investment market as an important growth area. In 1998, Friends Provident increased both its Marketing and Research capabilities to include the creation of a new Ethics Unit to complement the research commissioned from EIRIS. The unit increases Stewardship's ability to influence companies by increasing the number of people who engage with companies. This activity complements the previous better known aspects of the Stewardship funds – the extensive positive and negative screening criteria that are applied to every investment.

Contact Craig Mackenzie or Julia Dreblow, the Ethical Investment Marketing Consultant (0345 573 157; E-mail julia.dreblow@friendsprovident.co.uk) for additional information.

Friends, Ivory and Sime
15 Old Bailey, London EC4M 7EF
Contact: Neil Osborne
Tel: 0171 778 1145 *Fax:* 0171 236 2060
E-mail: n.osborne@friendsprovident.co.uk

FIS has a fourteen-year track record in ethical investment and now manages around £31 billion of ethically screened client assets on behalf of Friends Provident and for a number of institutional investment clients. Eleven UK local authorities have chosen to invest ethically with FIS, either on a segregated or a unitized basis, making it the market leader in this sector.

FIS has the capacity to provide a range of ethical investment opportunities to trustee and other institutional investors.

Henderson Investors
3 Finsbury Avenue, London EC2M 2PA
Contact: Kate Murphy
Contact's title: Fund Manager
Tel: 0171 638 5757 *Fax:* 0171 638 5742

Henderson Investors is a global asset manager with over £340 billion under management. Approximately £3180 million is run on behalf of charities, private clients and retail customers with an ethical brief. All of these focus *on avoiding investment in companies which break pre-determined criteria covering arms, pollution and human rights. These also seek to encourage companies committed to sustainability, fair trade, and a positive approach to their employees and customers. Henderson Investors act as a research team dedicated to ethical research who maintain dialogue with companies.*

Jupiter Asset Management

Jupiter Environmental Research, 1 Grosvenor Place, London SW1X 7JJ
Contact: Emma Howard Boyd
Contact's title: Head of the Jupiter Environmental Research Unit
Tel: 0171 412 0703 *Fax:* 0171 412 0705
E-mail: ehowardboyd@jupiter-group.co.uk *or* green.dept@jupiter-group.co.uk

Jupiter Asset Management, a subsidiary of Jupiter International Group, has been managing environmentally screened investments for over ten years. Products include the Jupiter Ecology Fund (launched in 1988), a unit trust, and the Jupiter International Green Investment Trust (launched in 1989). The group also manages the Skandia Ethical Managed Fund and the Lincoln Green Fund. It also provides a segregated green and ethical investment service for private and institutional clients.

Jupiter's primary motive remains the attainment of good investment results for its clients. Investment decisions are made by our specialist Fund Management Team, Simon Baker and Louise Johnson-Hill, who are guided by Jupiter's in-house Environmental Research Unit's three members of staff, Emma Howard Boyd, Charles Millar and Michael Tyrell. They are dedicated to the in-depth assessment of companies' environmental and social performance, with an emphasis on positive corporate behaviour.

The Research Unit places particular importance on engaging with company management during the research process. Through questionnaires, discussions, meetings and on-site visits, the Research Unit builds up a detailed picture of a company's environmental and social performance and is able to encourage measures for positive improvement.

Jupiter's Green Department meets quarterly with its Advisory Committee, made up of environmental specialists, who review companies approved by the Research Unit, offer advice on emerging environmental and social trends and guide the development of research methodology.

M & G Group plc

7th Floor, 3 Minster Court, Great Tower Street, London EC3R 7XH
Contact: Frank Blighe
Contact's title: Investment Product Manager
Tel: 0171 626 4588 *Fax:* 0171 623 8615

E-mail: frank_blighe@mandg.co.uk
Web: www.mandg.co.uk

M & G has managed charitable funds since 1960 and is one of the largest and most experienced providers in this field. We have been appointed by a number of institutional clients to manage portfolios using ethical or environmental criteria. These funds add up to several hundreds of millions of pounds. We are able to meet the needs of pension funds, charities and other institutional investors who are concerned about where their money is invested. M & G does not offer ethically or environmentally screened funds for individual investors.

Merrill Lynch Global Asset Management
Milton Gate, 1 Moor Lane, London EC2Y 9HA
Contact: Alan Albert

Merrill Lynch is a major financial institution. Among its diverse interests, it is a leading manager of charity funds in the UK.

Murray Johnstone
7 West Nile Street, Glasgow G1 2PX
Contact: Andrew Preston
Contact's title: Head of Ethical Investment
Tel: 0141 226 3131 *Fax:* 0141 221 5632
E-mail: apreston@murrayj.com

Murray Johnstone has for several years provided clients with an ethical investment option. In the UK, this has been limited to institutions and charities but, for United States investors, we also manage a pooled fund, the Calvert World Values International Equity Fund (CWVF). The CWVF is the largest and also the first ethically screened international mutual fund to be offered to individuals in the United States.

The investment criteria for the CWVF were developed jointly with the Calvert Group, one of the leading ethical investment groups in the United States. Our objective is to invest in financially sound companies operating with integrity towards their customers, employees, the local community and the environment. The fund seeks to avoid investing in companies associated with unhealthy products and services or poor records on human rights, labour relations and the environment. Murray Johnstone has been working closely with Calvert since the inauguration of the Calvert World Values International Equity Fund in 1992, in applying the criteria and developing it for new investment areas. We plan to offer a similar pooled investment fund to investors in the United Kingdom in 1999.

NPI Asset Management Limited

PO Box 227, 48 Gracechurch Street, London EC3V 0EJ
Contact: Mark Campanale
Contact's title: Investment Marketing Manager
Tel: 0171 623 4200 *Fax:* 0171 665 3301
E-mail: Mark_Campanale@npi.co.uk

NPI Asset Management Limited (NPIAM) provide investment management services to both the retail and institutional market. With an enviable performance track record in the management of ethical funds and segregated charity and private client portfolios that observe socially responsible investment criteria, the experience of the Global Care team helps Trustees achieve competitive performance returns whilst ensuring that their portfolios reflect the aims, objectives and beliefs of their organization.

Since 1988, the team of specialist investment managers and analysts has established an international reputation for their commitment to original research analyzing environmental, social and financial aspects of corporate activity. The team works together to identify investment opportunities and maintain a proprietary database of around 1300 companies worldwide. All companies whose stocks are purchased for socially responsible investment portfolios are fully researched, contacted and visited to make sure that the stocks meet both investment and ethical criteria. This double hurdle produces a universe of high quality stocks that have the potential to achieve consistently superior earnings growth.

Scottish Equitable

Edinburgh Park, Edinburgh EH12 9SE
Contact: Charles Henderson
Contact's title: Research Manager – Ethical Funds
Tel: 0131 549 3401 *Fax:* 0131 304 3460
E-mail: crhenderson@scoteq.co.uk

The ethical funds are managed by Scottish Equitable Asset Management (SEAM), the investment arm of Scottish Equitable plc.

SEAM offers two types of ethical vehicles:

The Ethical Care Funds seek to invest in companies which demonstrate socially and environmentally responsible behaviour or whose activities are for the benefit of humanity and the environment. They invest on the basis of positive criteria with some negative criteria and are designed to appeal to investors with broad-based ethical concerns and a desire to invest positively. Within this range, the Ethical Care Equity funds are available as a Pension Fund, a Performance Bond and a Unit Trust. The Ethical Care Cautious

Managed Fund, which invests in both equities and corporate bonds, is available through a Performance Bond only.

The Ethical Funds select companies on the basis of strict negative criteria and are therefore suited to investors who wish to avoid company activities to which they are opposed. This range comprises a Pension Fund, a Performance Bond and a Unit Trust.

Standard Life Assurance Company
Standard Life House, 30 Lothian Road, Edinburgh EH1 2DH
Contact: Gerry McGrath
Contact's title: Marketing Development
Tel: 0131 245 6097 *Fax:* 0131 245 5317
Web: www.standardlife.com

The Standard Life Assurance Company currently offers two ways to invest ethically. The Pension Ethical Fund is available through a variety of Standard Life's pension products. In addition, Standard Life Investments offers an Ethical Fund as part of its wide range of investment funds.

Both of these funds exclude investments on the basis of negative criteria and favour those that meet the postive criteria as stated in the Ethical Policy. This policy is determined by our customers through research carried out with a large sample of IFAs and investors. Standard Life uses the services of an independent research company to determine which companies comply with the requirements of the Ethical Policy and has set up an Ethical Committee to ensure that the funds remain within the spirit of the policy.

VTZ Green Money for the Blue Planet
Bahnhofplatz 9, Postfach 6139, CH-8023 Zurich, Switzerland
Contact: Elisabeth Stern
Tel: +41 1226 45 45 *Fax:* +41 1226 45 45

VTZ Green Money for the Blue Planet is located in Zurich. A pioneer in 'green' financial services since the early 1990s, the company has specialized in creating and placing environmentally sound financial products with private and institutional investors

For every conventional type of financial investment, we offer our customers green alternatives; our products range from stocks and bonds, life insurance policies and pension plans to renewable energy installations and real estate. VTZ is also playing a leadership role in the area of green venture capital, especially in energy-saving technologies; we are actively engaged in building up the network of green entrepreneurs and green investors in Europe and the United States.

OTHER ETHICAL FUND
MANAGEMENT GROUPS

....

Not all ethical fund managers are listed as members of EIRIS or UKSIF and so included below are other fund managers operating at the time of writing. It is more than likely that, by the time you read this, some of those listed will have merged with or been taken over by others and that there will be even more management groups in this market and so I can only repeat the facts that EIRIS, UKSIF or an IFA who works in this area will be able to provide up-to-date information.

Abbev Life Investment Services Ltd
Abbey Llfe Centre,
100 Holdenhurst,
Bournemouth
BH8 8AL
Tel: 01202 292373

Abtrust Unit Trust Managers Ltd
10 Queen's Terrace
Aberdeen
AB10 1QG
Tel: 01224 633070

Albert E. Sharp
Temple Court
35 Bull Street,
Birmingham
B4 6ES
Tel: 0121 200 2244

Allchurches Investment Management Services Ltd
Beaufort House
Brunswick Road,
Gloucester
GL1 1JZ
Tel: 01452 305958

CIS Unit Trust Managers Ltd
PO Box 105,
Manchester
M4 8BB
Tel: 0161 837 5060

City Financial Trust Managers Ltd
City Financial Centre
88 Borough High Street
London
SE1 1ST
Tel: 0171 556 8800

Commercial Union Plc.
1 Undershaft,
London
EC3P 3DQ
Tel: 0171 662 6017

Clerical Medical Unit Trusts Managers Ltd
Narrow Plain,
Bristol
BS2 OJH
Tel: 01275 554711

Credit Suisse Investment Funds (UK) Ltd
Beaufort House,
15 St. Botolph Street,
London
EC3A 7JJ
Tel: 0171 426 2929

Equitable Life Assurance Society
City Place House,
55 Basinghall Street,
London
EC2V 5DR
Tel: 0171 606 6611

Framlington Unit Management Ltd
155 Bishopsgate,
London
EC2M 3FT
Tel: 0171 374 4100

Homeowners Friendly Society Ltd.
PO Box 94,
Gardner House,
Hornbeam Park Avenue,
Harrogate
HG2 8XE
Tel: 01423 844000

Lincoln
Barnett Way
Barnwood,
Gloucester
GL4 3RZ
Tel: 01452 371371

Merchant Investors Assurance
St. Bartholomew's House
Lewins Mead
Bristol
BS1 2NH
Tel: 0117 926 6366

Sovereign Unit Trust Managers Ltd
Tringham House,
Wessex Fields,
Deansleigh Road,
Bournemouth
BH7 7DT
Tel: 01202 435000

TSB Unit Trusts Ltd
Charlton Place,
Andover,
Hants
SP10 1RE
Tel: Q1264 345678

United Charities Ethical Trust
16 West Street
Brighton,
East Sussex
BN1 2RE
Tel: 01273 725272

INDEX